Country Fare for City Folk

by Cathy Sillman
Cover illustration by Carla Cruttenden

Fuzzy Tekky Press—Palo Alto

Cover illustration by Carla Cruttenden

Divider page illustrations by Kenny Harris

Text illustrations by the students at San Jose State University's advanced illustration class taught by Professor Bunny Carter, fall semester of 1991.

Country Fare for City Folk
Copyright © 1993 by Cathy Sillman
All rights reserved. No portion of this book may be reproduced, either electronically, mechanically or by photocopying, without written permission of the publisher.

Additional books are available directly from the publisher for $14.95 plus $2.95 for tax and shipping.

Fuzzy Tekky Press
615 Bryson Avenue
Palo Alto, California 94306

ISBN: 0-9635565-0-9 : $14.95
Text design by Cathy Sillman and Bill Lynch
First Printing June 1993
Printed in the USA by Elite Design
on recycled paper with soy ink

To Bill

Contents

Contents 5
Introduction 7
Acknowledgements 13
Breakfast 15
Soup 53
Salads 89
Sandwiches & "Fist Food" 115
Appetizers 143
Entrees 163
Sauces & Condiments 195
Desserts 223
Index 257

Introduction

Country Fare was born in August of 1987 in a small commercial district nestled in a residential area of Palo Alto. Our neighbors soon became our best patrons, dropping in for coffee and muffins in the morning and returning in the evening after a long work day to pick up our specialty dinners to take home. The local business people happen by practically daily to nourish themselves at lunchtime. Our favorite customers are the "regulars," people who need not even verbalize their orders. We automatically make Jack a tofu stir-fry, pack pumpkin muffins for Chuck to take to the hospital for his early morning rounds and give Ruthie a plateful of her beloved gingersnaps.

My intention for writing Country Fare for City Folk is to present the best-loved dishes from Country Fare Restaurant in an easy to recreate fashion. I have mentioned throughout the book if certain pre-made or purchased items can result in amazing shortcuts. Many of the recipes, as you will soon find, use basic ingredients that have been previously prepared.

A typical restaurant uses a copious quantity of similar ingredients for many different recipes and, therefore, relies on what is known in the industry as "prepped" items. This obviously expedites cooking chores tremendously! It is a real cost saver in the long run in terms of little waste of precious ingredients and time. Please note how many times certain sauces and other "prepped" ingredients are used in a myriad of unique recipes. The "prepped" ingredients often do dual duty for various parts of the same meal.

Since there is no good home cooking without fresh, inexpensive, that is to say local, produce, and no produce is more local than that grown in the backyard, it stands to reason present gardeners must be encouraged and new gardeners enlisted if we are to have a population of knowledgeable eaters. — Leslie Land, *American Wine and Food*, April 1988

I recommend keeping your larder stocked with staples such as canned beans, dried fruits, grains, flour, dried pasta, tomato juice, tamari sauce, olive and canola oils, garlic, onions and fresh fruit. Numerous recipes can be produced using a combination of these ingredients with the well placed addition of fresh vegetables, tofu, tempeh, chicken or fish. Pre-made ingredients such as hummus or orange-tamari sauce can enliven soups, dips, or sandwich spreads. Frozen pesto, marinara, roasted red pepper or white sauces can be thawed and used simply as pasta toppings or as ingredients in more complex dishes such as cannelloni, lasagne, or dinner omelettes. When preparing pie pastry, form a few extra shells, wrap them well, and store them in your freezer. Leftover breakfast staples such as scones, croissants and muffins can be well-used as components of bread pudding. Save all leftover vegetables for use in soups or quick vegetarian casseroles. Even cookies can serve double duty — as gingersnaps do in the spicy crust for pumpkin pie. Use you imagination and let you best cooking ideas flow!

I, personally, prefer vegetarian food to dishes prepared with animal products. Modern health authorities now concur that a vegetarian diet or one that uses meat as a side dish is most beneficial for good health and long life. Thomas Jefferson seems to have been a real visionary in this respect. Jefferson was a proponent of home gardens with self-reliance as his goal. He was known for lavish dinner parties in which he would present a dish of the first spring peas of the season harvested in his community. A skilled gardener, Jefferson knew the value of home-grown produce for flavor and purity.

I have lived temperately, eating little animal food, and that as a condiment for the vegetables, which constitute my principal diet. — Thomas Jefferson, 1630

I always encourage customers to shop at the local farmers market to pick up the best and freshest organic produce. Organic products are de riguer at Country Fare. I rely on them for freshness, purity and — most of all — full flavor not found much anymore in commercially grown products. In addition to buying produce from the small independent growers, try putting in a garden of your own. Most people who cook love to garden as well, since they value food as a form of sustenance, nurtured from the ground to the plate. A garden can be as simple as a planter of herbs surrounding a cherry tomato plant or a small grouping of tomato, pepper and eggplant bushes nestled amid your flower garden. The flavor of really fresh tomatoes from the vine or just-picked basil is incomparable! Experiment with the unusual varieties and really perk up your meals. Gold jubilee tomatoes make an aesthetically pleasing and extremely tasty marinara sauce. Cinnamon basil is delightful in marinara sauce and also negates the need for adding sweetener. These varieties and many more can be found in farmers markets and natural food stores, but nothing beats the taste of fresh-from-the-garden fare. You won't be disappointed!

A combination of the qualities of the scholar, the master cook, the painter, the gastronome, the sportsman and the pantologist, assisted by the skill of the bookmaker and etcher, will be required to compose the cookbook par excellence. — George Ellwanger, *Pleasures of the Table* 1903

My motto for cooking is "make life easy on yourself." Efficiency in the kitchen is the key, and quick and easy recipes help the cause. If your day is especially hectic or your dinner party is becoming more stressful than fun, pick recipes with minimal ingredients or which have many pre-made components. Always strive for felicity in your endeavor and you will find peace in your kitchen.

Our modern lives often are ruled by hectic schedules. Here in Silicon Valley, most people barely have time to take a breath, much less cook an entire meal. Country Fare Restaurant offers these harried and weary troopers a calm oasis in the midst of the hustle and bustle of a fast-paced technological society. This cookbook will hopefully offer an easy way for you to duplicate the most popular and least time-consuming recipes we cook for our valued customers. A complicated lifestyle demands simple cooking.

You will notice many quotations sprinkled throughout the book from famous people as well as those not well-known to all. These unfamiliar names are those of our customers who thoughtfully recorded their comments in the Country Fare Journals — blank books which are left on the tables at the restaurant for just that purpose.

One of these days I'm going to ask them where they get the recipes for the wonderful food they serve here-- fresh, imaginative and delicious! (Maybe the owner could put a few of the best recipes in a cookbook for us to buy.) — a customer

The trouble with most cookbooks is that they assume that people live the way they don't live. — Mrs. Appleyard

Acknowledgements

This book was written at the request of many of our loyal customers. Special thanks must go to MaryLou Fischer, whose constant badgering made this book a reality. Thanks also to Jules Greenblatt for his seasoned advice on desktop publishing and to Steve Russell for his thought-provoking questions and advice. To all of the people who asked about and anxiously awaited the publication of this cookbook, thank you for your enthusiasm and support.

Special thanks must be given to all of those who helped directly or indirectly with the production of this book:

To Lisa Ludwig, a good friend and enthusiastic restaurant customer, for her editing expertise;

To Bunny Carter, whose advanced illustration class at San Jose State University, fall semester of 1991, did the illustrations for the cover and recipes throughout the book;

To Kenny Harris for his wonderful portraits gracing the divider pages;

To Susan Russell for transcribing recipes on our computer during the early stages of the book;

To Terri Wuerthner who also did recipe transcription and publicity for the restaurant;

To Michelle Hertig, a supportive friend and expert public relations resource;

To Susan Russell, Esther Escudero, Victor Mendoza, Enrique Chavez, Gilda Casillas, Ana Salgado, and Silvia Gama -- Country Fare staff members who ran the restaurant competently and allowed me to work on the book;

To Bruce Thier for teaching me about restaurant business techniques, spreadsheets and self-confidence;

To Gale Kinzie for mentoring me in the culinary profession when I needed it most;

To Mom for teaching me everything she knows about food and cooking (a lot!) and for fostering my imagination. Mom is the most encouraging, supportive and insightful person I know and a great cook, too!;

To Dad for sharing his love of good food and cooking, and for exposing me to fine restaurants as a child;

And especially to Bill, my business- and life-partner whose belief in me made the restaurant possible. Bill's software expertise greatly improved the quality of my life as I worked on this book. He also was responsible for the text format of this book and tirelessly helped me edit this work while finishing his dissertation at Stanford. He is a rare gem and vastly appreciated.

Customers often ask me about my culinary training and are curious about my self-taught status. I can not completely take the credit for my talent because my interest in food was nutured when I was a very small person. My maternal grandmother, Nan, was a particularly accomplished cook who cultivated a love of good cooking and eating in our entire family. Nan sewed little aprons with dingle balls on the pockets for me and my sisters and pressed us into service in her kitchen when we were as tall as her countertops. My early cooking memories include cookie baking and preparing oven-fried chicken (see recipe) in Nan's spacious kitchen. I vividly remember her proud proclamation to my mom that I prepared the chicken all by myself. I must have been about five-years-old at the time and burst with culinary confidence from that day forward. Nan's zest for life and unconditional support prompted me to start a business embodying what she did best -- feed people!

Breakfast

Apple Crumb Muffins	18
Crumb Topping	19
Orange Poppyseed Muffins	20
Orange or Lemon Zest	21
Pumpkin Muffins	22
Persimmon-Ginger Muffins	23
Banana Walnut Muffins	24
Zucchini Muffins	25
Oatmeal Muffins with Fruit	26
Bran Raisin Muffins	27
Maple Pecan Rolls	28
Blueberry Turnovers	30
Gingerbread Waffles	32
Lemon Curd	33
Buttermilk Waffles	34
Blackberry Sour Cream Coffeecake	35
French Toast	36
Hawaiian French Toast	37
Pistachio French Toast	38
Pumpkin Pancakes	39
Oatmeal Pancakes	40
Buckwheat Pancakes	41
Blue Cornmeal Pancakes	42
White Bean Omelette	43
Smoked Turkey and Sweet Potato Hash	44
Breakfast Savory Cheesecake	46
Potato Pancakes	47
Scalloped Potatoes	48
Cashew Fried Rice	49
Crepes	50
Blintzes	51
Eggs Baked in a Tomato Nest	52

Breakfast

The popularity of cooked breakfast is a well-respected fact in the restaurant business. The challenge is to make delicious, nutritious and creative additions to our menu to keep our regular customers coming back. Some of the best received breakfast entrees are the specialty waffles and pancakes we prepare. Muffins, of course, are always favorites, and I have included Country Fare's most sought after flavors. We often try unconventional recipes for breakfast in the restaurant to encourage people to eat more heartily at that meal. Try cashew fried rice or vegetarian risotto with scrambled eggs or salmon croquettes with wild rice for a variation on a traditional breakfast theme.

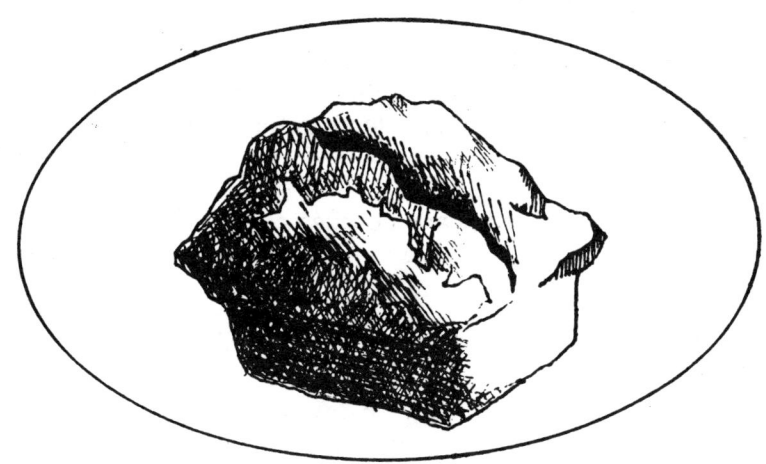

Apple Crumb Muffins
Makes 12 muffins

3 c.	unbleached flour
1 c.	brown sugar
4 tsp.	baking powder
1/2 tsp.	baking soda
1/2 tsp.	salt
2 tsp.	cinnamon
1/2 tsp.	allspice
4	eggs, beaten
2 c.	plain yogurt
1/2 c.	safflower oil
2 c.	apple, chopped
1/2 c.	crumb topping (see recipe next page)

Blend the first seven dry ingredients together. Beat together the eggs, yogurt and oil. Fold the dry ingredients into the wet ingredients and stir in the apples. Scoop the batter into paper-lined muffin cups and sprinkle with crumb topping. Bake at 400 degrees for 25 minutes.

Note: Use diced pears, peaches or plums for an inspired variation.

Breakfast

Crumb Topping

2 c.	walnuts, chopped
1 c.	unbleached flour
3/4 c.	brown sugar
1/2 c.	cold unsalted butter
1 tsp.	cinnamon

Grate the cold butter into the flour. Stir in the remaining ingredients. Refrigerate.

Orange Poppyseed Muffins
Makes 2 dozen muffins

1 1/2 c.	brown sugar
1/2 c.	safflower or canola oil
1 Tbsp.	orange zest, finely chopped (see recipe next page)
4	eggs, beaten
1 1/2 c.	buttermilk
1/2 c.	orange juice
4 c.	unbleached flour
1 tsp.	salt
5 tsp.	baking powder
1/2 tsp.	nutmeg
1 c.	dates, chopped
1 c.	pecans, chopped
1/2 c.	poppyseeds

Blend the wet ingredients together. Blend the dry ingredients together. Stir both mixtures together gently, then add the dates, nuts and poppyseeds. Bake at 400 degrees for 20 minutes in paper-lined muffin tins.

You don't get tired of muffins, but you don't find inspiration in them. — George Bernard Shaw

Breakfast

Orange or Lemon Zest

Wash the fruit rind well and peel large strips of the orange or lemon rind carefully to the depth of only 1/8 inch or the thickness of 4-5 sheets of paper. Do not peel any of the white pith, as it tastes bitter. Stack the thin peels of zest and slice carefully in julienne strips or chop finely for use in baked goods.

Pumpkin Muffins
Makes 24 muffins

5 c.	unbleached flour
2 tsp.	baking soda
4 tsp.	baking powder
2 tsp.	salt
2 c.	brown sugar
2 c.	pumpkin, cooked and pureed (or canned)
4	eggs, beaten
2 c.	buttermilk
1 c.	oil
1/2 tsp.	cinnamon
1/2 tsp.	nutmeg
1/4 tsp.	cloves

Blend the dry ingredients together. Blend the wet ingredients together. Add the dry ingredients into the wet ingredients and stir until just combined. Fill paper-lined muffin cups 3/4 full and bake at 400 degrees for 20 minutes.

Note: You may substitute peeled, cooked and mashed sweet potatoes for the cooked pumpkin. This recipe also translates well as a quick bread. Bake in a greased loaf pan, filled three-quarters full, for 50 minutes to one hour at 375 degrees.

Your sweet potato muffins are the best. Keep baking them. A very satisfied customer. Thank you

Persimmon-Ginger Muffins
Makes 12 muffins

5 c.	whole wheat flour
2 tsp.	baking soda
2 tsp.	baking powder
1 tsp.	salt
1/2 tsp.	cinnamon
1/2 tsp.	nutmeg
1/2 tsp.	cloves
1/2 c.	safflower or canola oil
2 Tbsp.	ground ginger powder
1 c.	honey
1/2 c.	brown sugar
1/2 c.	molasses
3	eggs, beaten
4 Tbsp.	lowfat plain yogurt
2 c.	fresh persimmon pulp, pureed

Blend the dry ingredients together. Blend the wet ingredients together. Combine both mixes and stir just until combined. Fill paper-lined muffin cups 3/4 full and bake at 400 degrees for 20-25 minutes.

Banana Walnut Muffins
Makes 12 muffins

2	eggs, beaten
1/2 c.	canola or safflower oil
2 c.	whole wheat flour
1 c.	brown sugar
3/4 tsp.	salt
1 tsp.	baking soda
2 tsp.	baking powder
1 c.	bananas, mashed
1/2 c.	walnuts, toasted and chopped

Combine the eggs and oil. Stir together the dry ingredients and add to the egg mixture. Add the bananas and walnuts and stir just until blended. Do not overmix! Fill paper-lined muffin tins 3/4 full and bake in a preheated 400 degree oven for twenty minutes or until brown.

Breakfast

A great use for all of that zucchini from the garden! This recipe may be baked in a greased loaf pan for an additional 25 to 35 minutes for an easy quick bread. Cover with foil if the top browns too quickly.

Zucchini Muffins
makes 1 dozen muffins

6 c.	all purpose flour
1 1/2 tsp.	salt
2 tsp.	baking soda
4 tsp.	baking powder
1 tsp.	cinnamon, powder
1/2 tsp.	ground ginger powder
3 c.	brown sugar
6	eggs, beaten
1 1/2 c.	canola or safflower oil
1 tsp.	vanilla extract
1 tsp.	orange juice
4 c.	zucchini squash, shredded
1 c.	pecans, toasted and chopped

Mix the dry ingredients together. Stir the wet ingredients together separately. Blend both wet and dry mixtures together. Fold in the zucchini and pecans. Portion the batter in paper-lined muffin tins 2/3 full. Bake at 400 degrees for 25 minutes or until golden brown.

Oatmeal Muffins with Fruit
Makes 12 muffins

1 c.	old-fashioned rolled oats
1 c.	buttermilk
1 c.	unbleached flour
1 tsp.	baking powder
1/2 tsp.	baking soda
1/2 tsp.	salt
1/4 c.	brown sugar
1	egg, beaten
4 Tbsp.	canola or safflower oil
1 c.	fresh berries or 1/2 c. jam

Combine the oats and buttermilk. Stir together the flour, baking powder and soda, salt and sugar. Add the egg and oil to the oats and stir in the dry ingredients only to blend. Fold in the fruit or jam carefully. Fill paper-lined muffin tins 3/4 full and bake in a preheated 400 degree oven for twenty minutes.

Oats: a grain which in England is generally given to horses, but which in Scotland supports the people. — Samuel Johnson, Dictionary of the English Language 1755

Bran Raisin Muffins
Makes 12 muffins

4	eggs, beaten
1 c.	canola or safflower oil
1 c.	molasses
6 c.	buttermilk
4 c.	whole wheat pastry flour
4 c.	wheat bran
8 tsp.	baking powder
2 tsp.	salt
2 c.	raisins

Blend the eggs, oil, buttermilk and molasses. Stir the dry ingredients together. Mix wet ingredients with the dry and add the raisins. Do not overmix! Bake in a preheated 400 degree oven for twenty minutes.

The kitchen is the great laboratory of the household, and much of the "weal and woe" as far as regards bodily health, depends on the nature of the preparations concocted within its walls. — Mrs. Isabella Beeton, The book of Household Management 1861

Maple Pecan Rolls
Serves 6

Pastry

1 c.	whole wheat pastry flour
1 c.	unbleached flour
2 1/2 tsp.	baking powder
1/4 tsp.	baking soda
1/4 tsp.	salt
3 Tbsp.	unsalted butter
1	egg, beaten
1 c.	buttermilk

Maple Pecan Filling

1/2 c.	brown sugar
1/2 c.	pecan halves
1/4 c.	melted butter
1/2 tsp.	ground cinnamon powder
2 Tbsp.	maple syrup

For the pastry:

Blend the dry ingredients together. Grate in the cold butter and blend gently. Carefully stir in the buttermilk and egg until well blended. Turn out onto a floured board and sprinkle well with flour (the dough will be sticky!). Fold the dough four times pressing well after each fold. Press the final fold into a rectangular shape and roll out to 1/2 inch thick.

For the filling:

Blend all of the filling ingredients together. Spread the filling evenly to the edges, leaving 1/2 inch bare at the top edge of the prepared pastry rectangle. Roll the pastry up like a jelly roll starting at the bottom short edge and finishing at the top. Pat into an even and fairly smooth cylinder. Slice into 1/2 inch portions, form into neat rounds and gently flatten. Place on a parchment paper-lined pan with two inch spaces between each pastry. Bake in a preheated 400 degree oven for twenty minutes or until lightly brown.

Note: Slice the baked rolls in half crosswise and dip in French toast batter. Let soak for 3 minutes or so before frying in butter on a hot griddle. This delectable dish — served with a touch of hot maple syrup — is known as Maple Swirl French Toast. Try it plain or with yogurt or sour cream.

Blueberry Turnovers
8 servings

2 pints	fresh blueberries, washed and drained
1 c.	fructose or sugar
1/2 tsp.	cinnamon
1/2 c.	tapioca starch or cornstarch
1 Tbsp.	cold unsalted butter, grated
1 1/2 lbs.	frozen puff pastry, thawed
1	egg, beaten with 1 Tbsp. water

Puree or mash half of the blueberries and blend them with the fructose, cinnamon and tapioca starch. Stir in the grated butter and whole blueberries. Divide the puff pastry into eight pieces and roll each on a floured board to rectangles approximately 4 inches by 6 inches. Place a spoonful of blueberry filling on the bottom half of the dough rectangle and brush the edges of the dough with the beaten egg. Fold the top half over the filling and press the edges to seal. Brush the top with the beaten egg and place on a baking tray lined with parchment paper. Continue with the remaining dough and filling. Bake the turnovers in a preheated 400 degree oven for twenty minutes or until golden brown and puffed. Cool the pastries and drizzle with parallel lines of glaze (recipe follows) if desired.

Glaze

    1 1/2 c.   confectioner's sugar
    1/4 c.   water

Blend sugar and water until very smooth. Put the mixture in a squeeze bottle or use a spoon to decorate the tops of the cooled pastries.

Note: Substitute fresh juicy summer fruits such as pitted cherries, sliced peaches, or plums. Remember to mash some of the prepared fruit to allow the juices to mix with the thickener.

These waffles are the favorite brunch entree at Country Fare. I promised Ruth that the recipe would be in the cookbook, and so here it is. Plan at least two hours to rest and read the newspaper after indulging in gingerbread waffles on Sunday morning.

Gingerbread Waffles
makes 1 dozen waffles

4 c.	all-purpose flour
1 Tbsp.	baking powder
2 tsp.	cinnamon
2 tsp.	ground ginger powder
1/2 tsp.	ground clove powder
1/2 tsp.	salt
1/2 c.	unsalted butter, softened
1 c.	brown sugar
1 c.	molasses
4	eggs, separated
2 c.	milk

Stir the dry ingredients together. Set aside. Blend the softened butter with the brown sugar and then add the molasses. Beat in the egg yolks one at a time. Carefully blend in the milk. Whip the egg whites until stiff. Fold the dry ingredients into the wet ingredients until just blended. Gently fold the whipped egg whites into the batter. Cook in a well buttered waffle iron about 4 minutes per side. Serve hot with lemon curd (see recipe next page) or with whipped cream and powdered sugar.

Note: Gingerbread waffles make a sweet and spicy base for an ice cream sundae. Top each waffle with a scoop of vanilla ice cream and a generous dollop of maple syrup.

Had I but a penny in the world, thou shouldst have it for gingerbread. — Shakespeare

Lemon curd is our all-time favorite ultra-rich decadent sauce. We slather it on scones or bake it in short crust dough for delectable lemon-raspberry tarts. Thinned with a little water or milk and heated until smooth, this recipe becomes a tasty sauce for waffles, pancakes or poached fruit. Try serving poundcake or fruitcake in a puddle of hot lemon curd for an outrageous treat.

Lemon Curd
makes 1 1/2 pints

1 Tbsp.	lemon zest, finely chopped
1/3 c.	lemon juice
3/4 c.	fructose
1/4 tsp.	salt
3	eggs, beaten
3	egg yolks, beaten
1/3 c.	cold unsalted butter, cut into small pieces

Place the lemon zest, juice, fructose, salt, whole eggs and yolks in the top of a double boiler. Keep the heat moderate and stir the mixture constantly until it thickens, about 10 minutes. Remove the sauce from the heat and stir in the cold butter cubes, one at a time, whisking thoroughly after each addition. Strain the lemon curd and chill. The lemon curd is delightful heated; however, you may need to add water to thin the sauce because it continues to cook and thicken after heating.

Buttermilk Waffles
Serves 6

2 c.	unbleached flour, sifted
1/4 tsp.	baking soda
1 1/2 tsp.	baking powder
1 Tbsp.	fructose or sugar
2	eggs, separated
1	vanilla bean, split lengthwise
1 tsp.	vanilla extract
1 3/4 c.	buttermilk
1/4 lb.	unsalted butter, melted
1/4 tsp.	salt

Sift flour with baking soda, powder and sugar. In a separate bowl, beat egg yolks until thickened. Scrape the vanilla seeds into the yolks. Stir in the vanilla extract, buttermilk and 6 Tbsp. of the melted butter. Add the liquid to the dry ingredients mixing with as few strokes as possible. Beat the egg whites with the salt until it forms soft peaks. Fold into the batter. Butter a waffle iron with the remaining melted butter and heat until hot. Drop batter in 4 ounce scoops in the waffle iron and cook for approximately three minutes per side or until crisply brown.

Last week I went to the state fair, but the Country Fare has better waffles! — Emily, age 8 Aug. 31, 1991

Blackberry Sour Cream Coffeecake

12 Hearty Servings — 9" cake pan

3/4 c.	unsalted butter, softened
1 c.	fructose or sugar
3	eggs
1 tsp.	vanilla
1 c.	sour cream or nonfat yogurt
2 1/2 c.	unbleached flour
3 tsp.	baking powder
1 c.	blackberry preserves
1 c.	crumb topping (see recipe page 19)

Blend the softened butter and sugar in a mixer until fluffy. Add the eggs one at a time, beating well after each addition, then add the vanilla. Add the sour cream and beat for one minute. Gently fold in the flour and baking powder. Butter a nine inch round cake pan. Place one half of the batter in the pan and spread carefully to the sides. The batter will be quite stiff. Dot the surface of the batter with half of the blackberry preserves and drop the remaining dough evenly over the preserves. Dot the last 1/2 cup of preserves over the dough and sprinkle all with the crumb topping. Bake in a preheated 375 degree oven for forty minutes.

French Toast
Serves 4

4	eggs, beaten
1 c.	milk
4 Tbsp.	sugar
1/2 tsp.	cinnamon
1 tsp.	vanilla extract
	pinch salt

Beat all ingredients together well. Dip 4 thick slices of bread in the batter and let them soak for a minute before frying them in hot melted butter or oil. Cook approximately three minutes per side.

Hawaiian French Toast
serves 4

1 Tbsp.	unsalted butter
1/2	ripe papaya, cut into chunks
1/4	ripe pineapple, cut into chunks
2	bananas, sliced
1/4 c.	coconut milk
8	thick slices whole grain bread

Cook the papaya and pineapple in a skillet in melted butter until the fruit releases its juice. Add the banana slices and cook until the fruit begins to thicken. Stir in the coconut milk and heat through. Serve this rich compote over grilled whole grain French toast (see recipe page 36).

Note: Canned coconut milk may be purchased in specialty food stores or in the Asian section of some grocery stores.

Pistachio French Toast
serves 2

  1 c.   raw, shelled pistachio nuts
  1 c.   French toast batter (see recipe page 36)
  4   thick slices whole wheat bread

Pulverize the pistachio nuts in a food processor or blender and place on a large plate. Soak the bread slices in the batter until all of the liquid is absorbed and dip each slice in the ground nuts to evenly coat both sides. Fry in butter for approximately 4 minutes per side and serve with warm maple syrup.

Note: Shelled pistachio nuts may be purchased in ethnic food stores specializing in Middle Eastern products.

I especially like to come for breakfast on Saturday mornings. Such a happy environment. — Earl

Breakfast

Pumpkin Pancakes
Serves 4

4	eggs
1 c.	milk
2 Tbsp.	clarified butter
1/4 c.	brown sugar
1 c.	whole wheat pastry flour
1 c.	fresh pumpkin, cooked and pureed (or canned)
1/4 tsp.	nutmeg
1/4 tsp.	cinnamon
2 tsp.	baking powder

Separate the eggs. Whip the egg whites until stiff peaks form. Blend the yolks, milk, butter, pumpkin puree, and brown sugar. Mix the dry ingredients together and blend into the wet mixture. Fold in the beaten egg whites gently. Fry on a hot buttered griddle for approximately three minutes per side. These pancakes are excellent with pecans. Sprinkle the tops of unturned pancakes with pecan halves and flip the pancakes to cook the nuts on the griddle.

For pottage and puddings and custard and pies Our pumpkins and parsnips are common supplies; We have pumpkin at morning and pumpkin at noon, If it was not for pumpkin, we should be undone. — American folk song, c. 1630

Oatmeal Pancakes
Serves 4

1	egg, beaten
1 1/2 c.	old-fashioned rolled oats
2 1/2 c.	milk
1/4 c.	canola or safflower oil
1 c.	whole wheat pastry flour
1 Tbsp.	brown sugar
1/2 tsp.	salt
1 tsp.	cinnamon
1 Tbsp.	baking powder

Blend the first four ingredients together and let soak for 10 minutes. Stir together the dry ingredients. Mix the wet and dry ingredients together. Fry spoonfuls on a hot buttered griddle for approximately five minutes per side.

Note: Sprinkle pitted, chopped dates and raw cashews on the pancake batter before turning to grill the second side.

The oat is the Horatio Alger of cereals, which progressed, if not from rags to riches, at least from weed to health food. — Waverley Root, Food 1980

Buckwheat Pancakes
Serves 6

3	eggs, beaten
2 c.	buttermilk
3 Tbsp.	clarified butter
3/4 c.	buckwheat flour
3/4 c.	whole wheat pastry flour
6 Tbsp.	rolled oats, powdered in a food processor or blender
3/4 tsp.	baking soda
1 1/2 tsp.	baking powder
3/4 tsp.	salt

Beat together the wet ingredients. Stir the dry ingredients together. Blend the wet and dry ingredients together. Place 4 ounce scoops of batter on a hot buttered griddle and cook approximately five minutes per side.

Blue Cornmeal Pancakes
serves 6

4	eggs
2 1/2 c.	buttermilk
1/3 c.	canola oil
2 1/4 c.	blue cornmeal
1/2 c.	whole wheat flour
1/3 c.	rolled oats, finely ground in a food processor or blender
1 tsp.	baking soda
2 tsp.	baking powder
1 tsp.	salt

Beat the eggs, buttermilk and oil together in a bowl. Stir dry ingredients together in a separate bowl. Blend the wet and dry ingredients together just until moistened. Ladle 1/4 c. of batter on a lightly-oiled griddle and cook for approximately three minutes per side or until golden brown.

Note: Serve blue cornmeal pancakes with grilled sausage or tempeh and plenty of warm maple syrup.

White Bean Omelette
4 servings

1 c.	small white beans
1	bay leaf
1 Tbsp.	clarified butter or safflower oil
1/4 c.	yellow onion, finely chopped
2	cloves garlic, minced
1 1/2 tsp.	salt
1/4 tsp.	black pepper
4 Tbsp.	clarified butter or safflower oil
12	eggs, beaten with 3 Tbsp. water
8 oz.	imported chevre (goat cheese from France is most delicious)
1/2 c.	roasted red pepper sauce (see recipe page 214)

Cover the beans with water and soak overnight. Drain, cover again with water, add the bay leaf and simmer for 1 1/2 hours.

Heat the butter and saute the onion and garlic briefly, taking care not to brown the garlic. Add the cooked, drained beans, salt and pepper. Keep warm while preparing the omelette.

Heat one tablespoon of the clarified butter in a large omelette pan. Add 1/4 of the beaten eggs and stir briskly until the eggs begin to set. Let the omelette set on the heat, shaking the pan occasionally to loosen the edges. When the omelette seems done, fill with 1/4 of the beans and 1/4 of the cheese. Fold the omelette onto a hot plate and keep warm in a low oven while preparing the remaining omelettes. Serve with a generous amount of red pepper sauce on top of each omelette.

Love and eggs are best when they are fresh. — Russian proverb

Smoked Turkey and Sweet Potato Hash

8 servings

2 c.	russet potatoes (about two medium), peeled and cut into 1/2 inch cubes
2 c.	sweet potatoes (about two medium), peeled and cut into 1/2 inch cubes
4 c.	smoked turkey, cut into 1/2 inch cubes
1/4 c.	canola or safflower oil
1 c.	parsnips, peeled and sliced
1 c.	carrot, peeled and sliced
3	green onions, sliced with 3 inches of the green tops
2 c.	poultry stock
1/4 tsp.	nutmeg powder
2 tsp.	salt
1/4 tsp.	black pepper
2 Tbsp.	fresh basil, chopped (or 1 Tbsp. dried)
2 Tbsp.	fresh oregano, chopped (or 1 Tbsp. dried)

Cook sweet potatoes in boiling water for fifteen minutes or until tender. Drain well. Cook russet potatoes in a separate pot of boiling water for ten minutes or until tender. Drain well. Saute the carrots, parsnips and yellow onion in the oil for five minutes or until tender. Add the sweet potatoes, russet potatoes, smoked turkey, green onion and poultry stock and simmer for thirty minutes or until most of the liquid has been absorbed. Stir in the salt, pepper and herbs right before serving. This hash is delicious served hot with poached eggs.

(continued)

Cookery is the art of preparing food for the nourishment of the body. Progress in civilization has been accompanied by progress in cookery. — Fannie Farmer, The Boston Cooking School Cookbook 1896

Breakfast

Note: Leftover smoked turkey hash can be reheated in a frying pan. Break an egg in the center and cover to steam through, about 3 minutes. This dish can also be cooked in a casserole in a 375 degree oven for 45 minutes.

Breakfast Savory Cheesecake
Serves 6

1/2 lb.	cream cheese
6	eggs
1/2 c.	unbleached flour
1 tsp.	baking powder
3/4 c.	milk
1/4 c.	melted butter
1 1/4 c.	ricotta cheese
2 1/2 c.	cheese, shredded (jack, cheddar or Swiss)
1/2 c.	fresh herbs, chopped (basil, oregano, parsley)

Beat cream cheese until fluffy in a mixer or food processor. Add the eggs, one at a time, and beat well. Stir in the milk, butter and ricotta cheese. Fold in the shredded cheese and herbs. Refrigerate for one hour (or overnight if baking the next morning). Stir the mixture before pouring in a buttered glass baking dish. Bake at 350 degrees for forty-five minutes. Cool for twenty minutes to let set up before cutting into wedges.

Note: This cheesecake makes a wonderful plan-ahead appetizer. Cut into thin wedges and serve napped with salsa fresca or roasted red pepper sauce (see recipe page 214).

For a spectacularly different pancake, substitute peeled sweet potatoes or yams for the red potatoes in this recipe.

Potato Pancakes
Makes 2 dozen pancakes

4 c.	red potatoes
2	eggs, beaten
1/4 c.	parsley, chopped
1 tsp.	salt
1/4 tsp.	white pepper
1/4 c.	unbleached flour
1/4 c.	potato starch

Grate the potatoes, rinse several times in cold water and drain well. Blend the rest of the ingredients together and mix with the potatoes. Fry 1/4 cup scoops on a hot buttered grill and flip when golden brown on the bottom. Cook several minutes to brown both sides.

Note: Serve potato pancakes with sour cream or lowfat yogurt and applesauce (see recipe page 218) or with cranberry catsup (see recipe page 216).

Scalloped potatoes may be prepared several days ahead and reheated for an elegant breakfast entree paired with grilled sausage or tempeh and scrambled eggs.

Scalloped Potatoes
Serves 8

8 c.	red potatoes, sliced thinly
1/2 c.	red onions, chopped
	salt and pepper to taste
4 Tbsp.	butter
1/2 c.	unbleached flour
1 c.	half-n-half
2 c.	milk
2 c.	cheddar cheese, grated

Cook the sliced potatoes in boiling water for 5 minutes. Drain well. In a buttered baking dish, layer 1/2 of the sliced potatoes. Sprinkle with salt and pepper and scatter with the chopped red onions. Sprinkle with 1/4 c. unbleached flour and dot with 2 Tbsp. of butter. Layer the remaining sliced potatoes, salt and pepper, sprinkle of flour and dot with the last 2 Tbsp. butter. Pour the milk and half-n-half evenly over the potatoes. Cover with foil and bake at 375 degrees for one hour. Remove the foil and scatter the grated cheese over the top of the potatoes. Put back into the oven uncovered to allow the cheese to brown, approximately thirty minutes more.

Cashew Fried Rice
serves 6

1/4 c.	peanut oil
4	eggs, beaten
2 Tbsp.	sesame oil
1 c.	green cabbage, shredded
1/4 c.	scallions, sliced
3/4 c.	cashew pieces, roasted
2	1/4 inch slices fresh ginger
2 Tbsp.	tamari or soy sauce
2 Tbsp.	sherry
1 1/2 c.	brown rice, cooked
1 1/2 c.	basmati rice, cooked

Scramble the eggs in hot peanut oil. Set aside and keep warm. Stir-fry the cabbage, scallions, cashews and ginger in hot sesame oil. Add remaining ingredients and heat through. Remove the ginger slices and stir in the cooked eggs. Serve hot.

Crepes

Makes 1 dozen crepes

1 1/2 c.	unbleached flour
1 tsp.	salt
2 tsp.	baking powder
4	eggs, beaten
3 c.	milk

Mix the dry ingredients together and set aside. Beat the eggs very well in a mixer. Add the milk and beat three minutes more. Blend in the dry ingredients. Strain through a fine mesh to remove any lumps. Pour 3 ounce scoops in a very hot buttered crepe pan or omelette pan and swirl quickly to coat the bottom of the pan with a thin layer of batter. Cook until tiny bubbles appear on the surface of the crepe. Flip over to brown the other side if desired (this step is not necessary if filling the crepes with a hot filling which will finish cooking the inside).

Note: The cooks at Country Fare find that they produce softer more uniform crepes when the batter is prepared and refrigerated overnight.

Blintzes

makes 1 dozen

3 c.	ricotta cheese
1/2 c.	brown sugar
1/2 tsp.	vanilla
1/2 tsp.	cinnamon
2	eggs, beaten
	pinch salt

crepes (see recipe previous page)

Blend all of the ingredients together well. Place 1/4 cup filling on the bottom edge of a cooked crepe. Fold the crepe up over the filling and pat lightly to flatten. Fold the sides of the crepe in to form straight parallel sides. Roll the filling over in the crepe twice to form a neat cylinder. Fry in hot butter for 3 minutes per side. Cover the blintzes after turning to steam heat them through.

Note: Serve blintzes with fresh berries or applesauce (see recipe page 218) and sour cream.

A spectacular brunch item that couldn't be easier to prepare. Serve with garlic toast and roasted potatoes.

Eggs Baked in a Tomato Nest
Serves 4

4	eggs
4	large tomatoes
2 Tbsp.	olive oil
1/2 lb.	mushrooms
2	green onions, sliced
2 Tbsp.	flour
1 1/2 c.	chicken stock, heated
	salt and pepper to taste

Hollow out the tomatoes, season with salt and pepper and bake for 10 minutes at 375 degrees. Heat the olive oil in a skillet and cook the onions and mushrooms for 4 minutes. Stir in the flour and cook an additional 3 minutes. Add the hot chicken stock and simmer for 15 minutes. Place each egg in each tomato and cover with the hot sauce. Bake for 20 minutes.

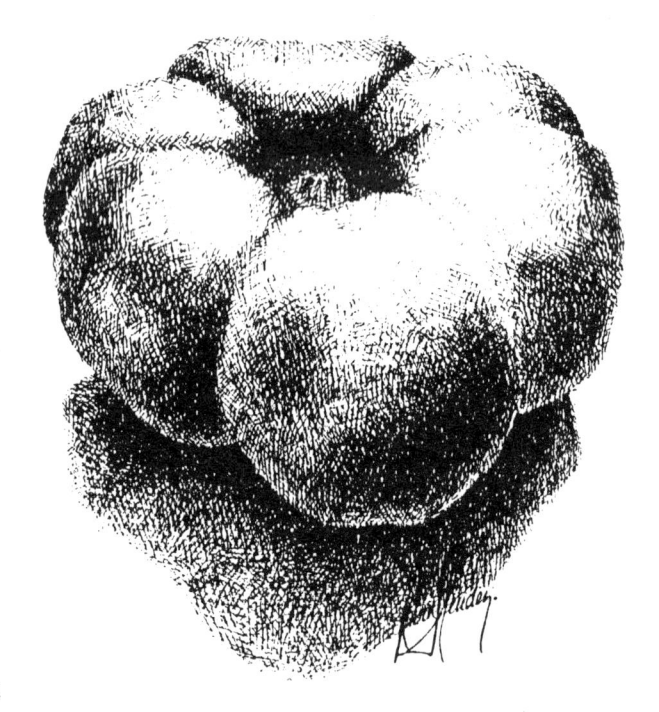

Soup

African Peanut Soup	56
Macho Gazpacho	57
Beet Borscht	58
Barley Mushroom	59
Miso Vegetable	60
Split Pea with Mint	61
Tomato with Wild Rice	62
Mediterranean Vegetable	63
Refried Beans and Cheese	64
Mushroom Noodle	65
Gingered Rice	66
Acorn Squash with Walnuts	67
Curried Tomato Vegetable	68
Barbecued Bean	69
Dahl	70
Lentil and Lovage	71
Spicy White Bean	72
Mexican Double Bean	73
Black-eyed Pea with Greens	75
Sherried Cream of Mushroom	76
Cream of Carrot with Amaretto	77
Cream of Pumpkin	78
Beer and Cheese Soup with Pecans	79
Cream of Spinach with Feta Cheese	80
Shrimp Bisque	81
Cream of Green Apple Soup	82
Succotash Soup	83
Creamy Turkey Garbanzo	84
Turkey Black Bean	85
Turkey Stuffing Soup	86
Navy Bean with Smoked Chicken	88

Soup

My favorite food to prepare, by far, is soup. Nourishing, nurturing and comforting best describe this steaming bowl of sustenance. Its many hours of simmering embody the care taken of the diner. A soup pot is the blank canvas in which an artist's palette of ingredients is used to create a masterpiece every time.

Most soups keep well covered in the refrigerator for a week or more. The exceptions are cream soups or those which contain seafood. These soups should be eaten within the week. Many soups freeze well, although cream soups may need to be pureed upon defrosting to return their previous silken texture. Almost every soup benefits from being prepared the day before they are to be served, to allow the flavors to marry overnight. I've discovered that this is especially true of bean soups. Cream soups, however, should be eaten almost immediately after cooking to prevent the white sauce from "breaking" or separating, which will occur if a cream soup is reheated at too high a heat.

I love the flavors of butter and milk in a creamy soup, but there are alternatives for those who are restricting their intake of dairy products and fat. Quite acceptable substitutes for dairy products are soy margarine and soy milk, which can be purchased in natural food markets and some conventional grocery stores. Prepare a white sauce using the same techniques of creating a roux with soy margarine and flour, and whisking in hot soy milk. For those avoiding fats, stir in pureed cooked rice, potatoes, tapioca or oatmeal into a finished soup to add creaminess. Traditional thickeners such as arrowroot, cornstarch or tapioca flour can also be used to thicken, but they will not add the same wonderful velvety texture.

African peanut soup was inspired by a vat of leftover spicy peanut sauce that we served with chicken satay as the daily special. This recipe is most tasty served the next day or when made with leftover peanut sauce (see recipe page 208). Just add stock, juices, onion and cilantro to your leftover satay sauce for a quick and delicious accompaniment to lunch or dinner.

African Peanut Soup
8 servings

1 Tbsp.	unsalted butter
1 c.	yellow onion, pureed in a food processor or blender
1	cloves garlic, minced
1/2 c.	peanut butter
1/4 c.	tamari or soy sauce
1/4 c.	brown sugar
1 Tbsp.	crushed red chilies
1 c.	orange juice
1/4 c.	lemon juice
4 c.	peanuts, toasted
6 c.	boiling water or hot stock
1/4 c.	fresh cilantro, chopped

Heat the butter until melted and saute the onion puree and garlic for five minutes. Stir in the peanut butter, tamari, brown sugar, chilies and juices. Puree the toasted peanuts in a food processor or blender with approximately two cups of the boiling water or stock. Add this peanut paste to the soup and stir in the remaining water to achieve a creamy, smooth consistency. Add the chopped cilantro just before serving.

"A note to all customers: One of my last meals in the Bay Area had to be "Country Fare." This is a great place folks, pay attention! People who prepare your food that care deeply about your health are few and far between--let alone those that care for the earth's health as well! Trust her, love her food, and enjoy!" — Sharon an ex-Country Fare "cookie"

Soup

This is like liquid salsa! Pair macho gazpacho with quesadillas or burritos for a satisfying lunch.

Macho Gazpacho
4 servings

1/4 c.	yellow onion, minced
1/2 c.	celery, minced
1/2 c.	cucumber, peeled, deseeded and minced
1/2 c.	bell pepper, deseeded and minced
2	cloves garlic, crushed
1/2	jalapeno pepper, minced (we leave the seeds in for heat, judge this for yourself)
1/4 c.	lemon juice
1/4 c.	picante salsa (bottled is fine)
1/4 c.	cilantro leaves, minced
1 tsp.	salt
1/4 tsp.	white pepper
4 c.	tomato or vegetable juice
1/4 c.	plain yogurt or sour cream, optional
2 Tbsp.	cilantro leaves, optional

Blend ingredients well and chill to marry the flavors. Serve with a spoonful of yogurt or sour cream and cilantro leaves.

I am amazed at the polarized response to borscht. People either swoon with delight over beets, or they despise them. However, even some confirmed beet-haters like Country Fare's borscht. Serve borscht and piroshki together for an authentic Russian lunch.

Beet Borscht
8 servings

6	large beets (about 1 lb.)
8 c.	water
2 Tbsp.	unsalted butter
1 Tbsp.	extra virgin olive oil
2 c.	carrots, peeled and sliced
2 c.	green cabbage, shredded
4	cloves garlic, crushed
1/2 c.	yellow onion, finely chopped
1/2 c.	lemon juice
2 Tbsp.	raspberry vinegar
1/2 c.	fructose or honey
1/2 c.	tomato paste
1 1/2 tsp.	salt
1/2 tsp.	white pepper
1/4 c.	dill, minced
1/2 c.	sour cream

Scrub the beets and cover them with the 8 cups of water in a large pot. Bring to a boil and simmer for forty-five minutes, or until beets are tender. Cool the beets in their liquid (save all of the liquid). When the beets are cool enough to handle, peel them (the skins slip off easily) and chop them into 1/2 inch cubes. Set the cubed beets aside.

Heat the butter and olive oil together and saute the vegetables until the onions are translucent. Stir in the beet liquid, lemon juice, vinegar, sweetener, tomato paste, salt and pepper. Simmer the soup for forty-five minutes to blend the flavors. Right before serving, add the chopped beets and dill and heat to warm through. Serve topped with sour cream.

A warming winter classic.

Barley Mushroom
8 servings

2 c.	pearl barley
6 c.	vegetable or chicken stock
1 Tbsp.	canola or safflower oil
1/2 c.	yellow onion, finely chopped
1/2 c.	celery, finely chopped
1/2 c.	carrot, peeled and grated
4 c.	white mushrooms, thinly sliced
1/4 c.	sherry
2 Tbsp.	tamari or soy sauce
2 tsp.	salt
1/4 tsp.	white pepper
4 c.	stock or water
1/4 c.	mixed fresh herbs, minced (we use parsley, dill and oregano)

Cook the barley in the stock for about one hour or until most of the liquid is absorbed. Heat the oil and saute the vegetables for two minutes, then cover the pan to steam them until crisp-tender. Add the sherry, tamari, salt, pepper and stock. Stir in the barley and its remaining liquid. Cook until heated through. Stir in the fresh herbs just before serving.

The easiest soup by far! Use up cooked leftover vegetables, rice or noodles to make a quicker version of this soup.

Miso Vegetable
6 servings

2 Tbsp.	canola or safflower oil
1/4 c.	yellow onion, finely chopped
1/4 c.	celery, finely chopped
1/4 c.	carrots, peeled and chopped
1/4 c.	zucchini, chopped
1/4 c.	bell peppers, chopped
1/4 c.	cauliflower, chopped
1/4 c.	broccoli, chopped
1/4 c.	green onions, sliced thinly
1 c.	white mushrooms, sliced thinly
1 c.	miso, any flavor
6 c.	water or vegetable stock

Heat the oil and saute the vegetables for two minutes. Cover the pan to "sweat" the moisture out of them for approximately ten minutes. Blend the miso with one cup of stock or water and stir into the tender vegetables. Add the remaining stock or water and simmer gently until hot. Do not bring to a boil, as this cooks the nutrients out of the delicate miso. (Traditionally, miso is added just before serving, but I like the vegetables to absorb the miso flavor.)

Split Pea with Mint
10 servings

2 Tbsp.	canola or safflower oil
1/2 c.	yellow onion, minced
1/2 c.	celery, minced
1/2 c.	carrots, peeled and grated
4	cloves garlic, minced
3 c.	split peas, rinsed well
8 c.	water or stock
2	bay leaves
2 tsp.	salt
1/2 tsp.	white pepper
1/4 c.	fresh mint, minced

In a large soup pot, heat the oil and saute the vegetables for ten minutes. Add the peas, water and bay leaves and bring to a rolling boil. Reduce the heat and simmer, stirring often, for forty-five minutes or until the peas are quite soft. Add the salt, pepper and mint and simmer gently until the soup is soft and creamy. Garnish with fresh mint leaves.

To make a good soup, the pot must only simmer, or "smile."—French proverb

Tomato with Wild Rice
6 servings

1 Tbsp.	canola or safflower oil
1/2 c.	yellow onion, minced
1/2 c.	celery, minced
1/2 c.	carrot, peeled and minced
3	cloves garlic, minced
1 c.	wild rice
2 c.	water or stock
4 c.	tomato or vegetable juice
1 c.	marinara sauce (see recipe page 206)
1 tsp.	salt
1/4 tsp.	white pepper
1/4 c.	mixed herbs, minced (dill, parsley and basil are a nice combination)

Heat the oil and saute the onion, celery, carrots and garlic until just barely cooked, about five minutes. Add the rice and water and cook, covered, for approximately forty-five minutes or until the liquid is absorbed. Add the juice, sauce, salt and pepper and heat through. Stir in the herbs just before serving. Garnish with plain cooked brown rice or toasted croutons.

This should actually be called ratatouille soup because of its origin. To make your own version of this soup, cut up leftover ratatouille (see recipe page 167) and add your favorite marinara sauce (see recipe page 206)and stock.

Mediterranean Vegetable
12 servings

1/2 c.	extra virgin olive oil
1/2 c.	yellow onion, finely chopped
1	medium eggplant (about 1 lb.), peeled and diced
4	cloves garlic, crushed
2 c.	zucchini, diced
1 c.	bell pepper, diced
2 c.	tomatoes, deseeded and diced
6 c.	tomato or vegetable juice
1 c.	white wine
2 c.	water
2 tsp.	salt
1/4 c.	fresh oregano, chopped
1/4 c.	fresh basil, chopped
1/4 c.	fresh parsley, chopped
1/2 c.	Parmesan cheese, optional
1 c.	salad croutons, optional

Heat the olive oil and saute the onions and garlic until translucent. Add the eggplant and cook, stirring frequently, until the cubes soften. Stir in the zucchini and peppers. cover and steam the vegetables for ten minutes, checking periodically to prevent scorching. Add the tomatoes, juice, wine, water and salt and simmer for forty-five minutes or longer. Stir in the fresh herbs just before serving. Garnish with the croutons and cheese, if desired.

This soup is a simple use of leftover refried beans. Pair it with cornbread or tortilla chips for an extremely filling lunch. A little goes a long way!

Refried Beans and Cheese

2 c.	pinto beans, cooked in 6 c. water for one hour
2 Tbsp.	olive oil
1 c.	yellow onion, finely chopped
6	cloves garlic, crushed
2 c.	bell peppers, finely chopped
1	jalapeno pepper, deseeded and chopped
4 c.	water or stock
2 c.	Monterey jack cheese, grated
2 tsp.	salt
1/2 tsp.	white pepper
1 tsp.	cumin powder
1/8 tsp.	cayenne pepper
3 dashes	Tabasco sauce

Mash one half of the cooked beans and add back to the whole beans and their cooking liquid. Saute the onion, garlic, peppers and jalapeno in the olive oil for ten minutes. Add the vegetables to the beans along with the water or stock, cheese and spices. Simmer gently to melt the cheese and heat throughout. Garnish with more grated cheese and chopped olives.

Mushroom Noodle
8 servings

6 c.	mushrooms, thinly sliced
1/2 c.	red onion, finely chopped
1/2 c.	celery, finely chopped
2	cloves garlic, minced
1 Tbsp.	olive oil
1/2 c.	traditional red miso
6 c.	water or stock
1/4 c.	chives, snipped
1/4 c.	dill, minced
1 c.	fettucine noodles, cooked in 3 c. boiling water until *al dente*, then drained

Saute the mushrooms, onion, celery and garlic in olive oil. Add the stock or water and bring to a boil. Turn off the heat and stir in the miso, herbs and noodles.

Gingered Rice
8 servings

1 c.	raw long-grain brown rice, cooked in 2 c. water
1/2 c.	yellow onion, finely chopped
1/2 c.	carrots, peeled and grated
1/2 c.	parsnips, peeled and grated
1/2 c.	cauliflower, finely chopped
1 tsp.	canola or safflower oil
1 c.	tomato or vegetable juice
6 c.	stock or water
1/2 c.	traditional red miso
2 Tbsp.	fresh ginger, peeled and grated
1 Tbsp.	tamari or soy sauce

Saute the onion, carrot, parsnip, and cauliflower in the oil. Stir in the juice, stock, ginger and tamari and bring to a boil. Lower the heat and stir in the miso and cooked rice. Let simmer just to heat through. Garnish with toasted sunflower seeds or toasted chopped peanuts.

Acorn Squash with Walnuts
8 servings

2	medium acorn squash, cut in half and seeds removed
1 c.	walnut pieces, toasted and chopped
1 Tbsp.	canola or safflower oil
1 c.	yellow onion, finely chopped
6 c.	water or stock
1/2 c.	brandy
1/2 c.	tart green apple, peeled and chopped
2 tsp.	salt
1/2 tsp.	cracked pepper
1/4 tsp.	cinnamon powder
1/4 tsp.	nutmeg powder

Place the squash cut side down on a baking sheet. Bake in a preheated 400 degree oven for one hour. Scoop out the soft pulp and mash or puree in a food processor or blender. Saute the onion in the oil until tender, about five minutes. Add the chopped apple to the onion and cook for five minutes more. Stir all the ingredients together in a heavy-bottomed pot and heat gently for thirty minutes to blend the flavors. Serve with additional chopped walnuts as a garnish.

Note: This soup is equally delicious when prepared with cooked pumpkin or butternut squash.

Curried Tomato Vegetable
8 servings

1 Tbsp.	clarified butter
1/2 c.	red onion, finely chopped
1/2 c.	celery, finely chopped
1/2 c.	carrots, peeled and grated
1/2 c.	cauliflower, chopped
1/2 c.	zucchini, grated
1 c.	red potatoes, washed and grated
1/2 c.	broccoli, chopped
1 Tbsp.	ginger, peeled and grated
6	cloves garlic, minced
1	jalapeno pepper, deseeded and minced
1/2 c.	brown rice, cooked in 1 c. water
4 c.	tomato or vegetable juice
2 c.	stock or water
2 tsp.	salt
1/2 tsp.	white pepper
1/8 tsp.	cayenne pepper
1 tsp.	cumin powder
2 tsp.	mild curry powder
1/4 tsp.	cinnamon powder
1/4 tsp.	nutmeg powder
2	dashes Tabasco sauce

Saute the garlic, jalapeno and ginger in the clarified butter. Add all of the vegetables and 2 c. of stock or water and braise until tender, about fifteen minutes. Stir in the tomato juice, rice and spices. Heat until piping hot. Garnish with yogurt mixed half and half with your favorite chutney.

True gastronomy is making the most of what is available, however modest. — Claudia Roden, Picnic 1981

This soup was developed when some excellent odds and ends were put together, and formed a soup people oohed and aahed over. The customers liked this soup so much, we had to freshly prepare the ingredients to recreate what started out as a way to use up leftovers.

Barbecued Bean
8 servings

2 Tbsp.	unsalted butter
2 c.	pinto beans, cooked in
4 c.	water for one hour
1/2 c.	yellow onion, finely chopped
4	cloves garlic, crushed
1/2 c.	celery, finely chopped
1/2 c.	carrots, peeled and grated
1/2 c.	bell peppers, finely chopped
6 c.	vegetable stock or water
1/4 c.	brown sugar
1/4 c.	molasses
1/4 c.	tamari or soy sauce
1/4 c.	cider vinegar
1 Tbsp.	salt
1/2 tsp.	white pepper
1/4 tsp.	cayenne pepper
1/2 c.	raisins, optional
1/2 c.	cooked rice, optional

Melt the butter and saute the vegetables until crisp-tender, about ten minutes. Add the beans and remaining ingredients and simmer for one hour or more to blend the flavors. Serve with a handful of raisins or hot cooked rice as a garnish.

Dahl

10 servings

4 c.	lentils (preferably red, but brown are fine)
10 c.	water
1	bay leaf
2 Tbsp.	unsalted butter
1/2 c.	yellow onion, finely chopped
4	cloves garlic, crushed
1	jalapeno pepper, minced
1 Tbsp.	fresh ginger, peeled and grated
1/2 c.	celery, finely chopped
1/4 c.	lemon juice
2 tsp.	cumin powder
2 tsp.	coriander powder
2 tsp.	tumeric
1 tsp.	white pepper
1/4 tsp.	cayenne pepper
1 tsp.	salt
3/4 c.	plain yogurt, optional
1/2 c.	chutney, optional

Cover the lentils with water and soak for several hours. Drain and add the ten cups of fresh water. Cook the lentils with the bay leaf for forty-five minutes. Remove the bay leaf. Melt the butter and saute the onion, garlic, jalapeno pepper, ginger and celery until soft. Stir onion mixture into the lentils with the lemon juice. Add the spices and simmer for one half hour to allow the flavors to meld. Mix the yogurt and chutney together and top each serving with two tablespoons of the mixture as a delicious garnish.

Soup

Lentil and Lovage
6 servings

2	bay leaves
2 c.	lentils, washed
6 c.	water or stock
1 Tbsp.	canola or safflower oil
1/2 c.	celery, minced
1/2 c.	yellow onion, finely chopped
1/2 c.	carrots, peeled and grated
2	cloves garlic, minced
1/4 c.	lovage or celery leaves, finely chopped
1/4 c.	parsley, finely chopped
1/2 c.	dry white wine
2 tsp.	salt
1/2 tsp.	white pepper

Cook the lentils and bay leaves in the water or stock and simmer for 45 minutes. Saute the celery, onion, carrots and garlic in the oil until crisp tender. Add the cooked lentils to the vegetables. Remove the bay leaves. Stir in the herbs, wine, salt and pepper. Add more liquid to your preference (more for a brothy soup and none for a thick stew-like soup) and simmer for 40 minutes.

A great way to stretch leftover chili! Add tomato juice or stock to white bean chili (see recipe page 179) and garnish with grated cheese and chopped olives.

Spicy White Bean
8 servings

2 c.	small white beans, cooked in 6 c. water for one hour
2	bay leaves
1 Tbsp.	olive oil
4	cloves garlic, crushed
2	jalapenos, deseeded and minced
1 c.	yellow onion, finely chopped
1 1/2 c.	sweet bell peppers, finely chopped
2 c.	tomatoes, deseeded and chopped
1 tsp.	salt
1/4 tsp.	cracked pepper
1/8 tsp.	cayenne pepper
1 tsp.	sweet paprika
1/2 c.	white wine
4 c.	stock or water

Simmer the cooked beans in their liquid with the bay leaves for thirty minutes more. Remove and discard bay leaves. Saute the garlic, jalapenos, onions and peppers in the olive oil until crisp-tender, about ten minutes. Stir in the tomatoes and cook, stirring frequently for five minutes. Add the beans, their cooking liquid, the spices and the additional stock or water and simmer for one half hour until hot. Garnish with cilantro sour cream(see recipe page 212).

Soup

As with all of the bean soups in this book, canned beans are quicker and easier to use than cooking dried beans from scratch. However, cooked beans have a myriad of culinary uses and leftovers will pose no problems for the creative cook. All beans are useful in lowering cholesterol by providing the body with delicious dietary fiber. Soak the beans overnight and rinse in fresh water before cooking.

Mexican Double Bean
8 servings

1 c.	pinto beans, cooked in 3 c. water for one hour
1 c.	black beans, cooked in 3 c. water for one hour
1 c.	yellow onion, finely chopped
1/2 c.	celery, finely chopped
1 c.	sweet green peppers, chopped
1 c.	tomatoes, deseeded and chopped
2	jalapeno peppers, deseeded and chopped
6	cloves garlic, crushed
1 Tbsp.	olive oil
6 c.	vegetable juice blend or tomato juice
1 tsp.	salt
1/2 tsp.	white pepper
1/8 tsp.	cayenne pepper
1/4 c.	cilantro, coarsely chopped
1/4 c.	oregano, coarsely chopped
2 tsp.	sweet paprika

(continued)

Drain the beans and set aside. The pinto bean liquid may be used in this soup, however the black bean liquid will turn the broth a muddy, unpleasant color and should be saved for black bean soup or watering the plants. Saute the onion, celery, peppers, jalapenos and garlic in the olive oil for five minutes. Add the tomatoes and cook five minutes more. Stir in the juice, spices and herbs. Simmer for approximately twenty minutes. Stir in the beans and heat until piping hot. Garnish with a dollop of herbed sour cream, yogurt or toasted pumpkin seeds.

Black-eyed Pea with Greens
8 servings

2 c.	black-eyed peas
6 c.	water or stock
1	bay leaf
1 Tbsp.	olive oil
1/2 c.	yellow onion, minced
4	cloves garlic, crushed
1/2 c.	celery, minced
1/2 c.	carrots, peeled and grated
2 c.	Swiss chard or kale, sliced in thin strips (chiffonade)
6 c.	water or stock
2 tsp.	salt
2 tsp.	cider vinegar
1/4 tsp.	cracked pepper
4	dashes Tabasco sauce

Cook the peas and bay leaf in the water or stock for one hour or until tender. Remove the bay leaf and discard. Saute the onion, garlic, celery and carrots in the olive oil for ten minutes. Add to the cooked peas and their liquid. Saute the greens (carefully to prevent scorching) until just wilted. Add to the peas with the additional water or stock, spices and vinegar. Simmer for twenty minutes to blend the flavors. Serve garnished with pureed, cooked greens.

Thank you for feeding us almost every day! — Charles and Jeannie Sept. 19, 1991

One of our customers gave us his telephone number and asked us to call him whenever we make sherried cream of mushroom soup. No matter how many gallons we make, we always run out of this one quickly.

Sherried Cream of Mushroom
8 servings

2 Tbsp.	unsalted butter
8 c.	sliced white mushrooms
1/2 c.	red onion, finely chopped
1/4 c.	tamari or soy sauce
1/4 c.	sherry
1/2 c.	unsalted butter
1/2 c.	unbleached flour
1 quart	milk, heated
1 tsp.	salt
1/2 tsp.	white pepper
1/4 tsp.	nutmeg powder

Melt the 2 Tbsp. of butter and saute the mushrooms and onions for ten minutes or until the mushrooms have released all of their liquid. Add the tamari and sherry and simmer for ten minutes to evaporate the alcohol. Make a roux by melting the 1/2 c. butter and add in the flour, stirring frequently for seven minutes. Stir in the hot (not scalded!) milk, whisking constantly to create a thick white sauce. Add the seasonings to the sauce and blend with the sauteed mushrooms, adding more milk or water if necessary to thin the soup. Serve hot and often (our customers are happy to stand in line for this soup).

Nature alone is antique and the oldest art a mushroom. — Thomas Carlyle

Cream of Carrot with Amaretto
10 servings

1/4 c.	unsalted butter
1/4 c.	unbleached flour
2 c.	milk, heated
12	medium carrots, peeled and coarsely chopped
1/4 c.	yellow onion, sliced
4 c.	water
1/4 c.	Amaretto
1/2 tsp.	cinnamon
1/4 tsp.	nutmeg powder
1 tsp.	salt
1/4 tsp.	white pepper
5 Tbsp.	walnuts, toasted and chopped
5 Tbsp.	plain yogurt
1 Tbsp.	maple syrup

Make a roux by heating the butter until melted and add the flour, stirring constantly for five minutes. Add the hot milk and whisk quickly to form a thick white sauce. Simmer the carrots and onion in the water and Amaretto until very soft, about forty-five minutes. Puree the vegetable mixture in a food processor or blender until smooth. Stir the vegetable puree into the white sauce and add the spices. Heat until warmed through. Blend the yogurt and maple syrup and place a dollop of this mixture on each serving, then sprinkle each with chopped walnuts.

Of soup and love, the first is best. — Spanish proverb

Bake extra pumpkins when making pumpkin muffins or pumpkin pancakes and try this hearty autumn soup. Cut a sugar pie pumpkin in half and scoop out the seeds. Place the cut side down on a lined baking sheet and bake at 350 degrees for 45 minutes or until the pumpkin feel soft when pierced with a fork. Allow the baked pumpkin to cool, then scoop the flesh out of the skin.

Cream of Pumpkin
10 servings

1/2 c.	unsalted butter
1/2 c.	unbleached flour
4 c.	milk, heated
1 Tbsp.	unsalted butter, additional
1 c.	yellow onion, finely chopped
1/2 c.	brandy
8 c.	fresh pumpkin, cooked and pureed (canned is more convenient)
1 c.	water or stock
1 tsp.	salt
1/4 tsp.	white pepper
1/4 tsp.	nutmeg powder
3/4 c.	plain yogurt, optional
1/2	toasted pumpkin seeds, optional

Melt the butter until bubbly and add the flour. Simmer stirring constantly until thick and smooth. Stir in the hot milk and whisk quickly to form a thick white sauce. Saute the onion in the butter until transparent. Add the brandy to the onions and cook until the liquid is evaporated. Blend the white sauce, pureed pumpkin, onions and spices together and heat gently until hot. Garnish each serving with a dollop of yogurt and a sprinkling of pumpkin seeds.

Only the pure of heart can make a good soup. — Ludwig Van Beethoven

Beer and Cheese Soup with Pecans

8 hearty servings

1 Tbsp.	clarified butter or safflower oil
1 c.	yellow onion, minced
1 c.	leeks, thinly sliced
1 c.	fennel, thinly sliced
1 c.	celery, thinly sliced
3	cloves garlic, minced
4 c.	chicken or vegetable stock
1	12 ounce bottle of premium beer or ale
4 large	russet potatoes, peeled, boiled and mashed
2 tsp.	salt
1/4 tsp.	white pepper
1/4 tsp.	cayenne pepper
1/4 c.	fennel leaves, chopped
1/4 c.	celery or lovage leaves, chopped
1 c.	pecans, toasted and chopped
2 c.	cheddar or Swiss cheese, grated

Heat the butter or oil and saute the onion, leeks, fennel, celery and garlic together until crisp-tender. Add the stock and beer and bring to a boil. Stir in the mashed potatoes, salt, pepper, cayenne, fennel and celery leaves. Puree one half cup of the pecans with 1/4 c. of the soup and stir back into the pot. Heat until very hot throughout. Stir in the grated cheese and continue stirring until the cheese is melted. Garnish with the remaining chopped pecans.

Potato: bland, amiable, and homely, an honest vegetable, giving honour where honour is due--in an honest soup. — Della Lutes, The Country Kitchen 1938

A great use for leftover spanakopita filling, creamed spinach or wilted fresh spinach.

Cream of Spinach with Feta Cheese
8 servings

2 large	bunches of spinach, washed in several changes of water
1 Tbsp.	unsalted butter
1/2 c.	yellow onion, sliced
1/2 c.	unsalted butter, additional
1/2 c.	unbleached flour
4 c.	milk, heated
1/2 tsp.	white pepper
1/2 tsp.	nutmeg powder
1 c.	feta cheese, crumbled
1 c.	water or stock
1/2 c.	feta cheese, crumbled, additional

Steam the spinach in the water that clings to the leaves after washing. Heat the tablespoon of butter and saute the onion until transparent. Puree the cooked spinach and onion in a food processor or blender until smooth. Heat the half cup of butter until bubbling and add the flour, stirring constantly until smooth. Add the hot milk and whisk rapidly to form a thick white sauce. Add the pureed spinach mixture, pepper, nutmeg, the one cup of feta cheese and water. Heat gently. Serve with the additional feta cheese as a garnish.

Of all the items on the menu, soup is that which exacts the most delicate perfection and the strictest attention. —Escoffier

Launch an elegant dinner party with shrimp bisque as an appetizer. Serve each bowl with a small floating pastry boat filled with tiny bay shrimp.

Shrimp Bisque
12 servings

2 Tbsp.	unsalted butter
1/2 c.	yellow onion, finely chopped
1/2 c.	celery, finely chopped
2 c.	red potatoes, cut in 1/2 inch cubes with the skins
2	cloves garlic, crushed
1/2 c.	unsalted butter
1/2 c.	unbleached flour
8 c.	milk, heated
3/4 lb.	bay shrimp, cooked
2 tsp.	salt
1/2 tsp.	white pepper
1/4 c.	sherry
1/4 c.	tomato paste blended with 1/2 c. water
4 c.	tomatoes, deseeded and chopped
1/2 c.	dill, minced

Melt the butter and saute the onions, celery, potatoes and garlic until the potatoes are soft, about thirty minutes. (Add 1/2 c. water or stock to speed the process if desired.) Make a roux by melting the butter, stirring in the flour and cooking for five minutes stirring constantly. Add the hot milk and whisk quickly to form a white sauce. Stir in the vegetables and remaining ingredients and heat gently to prevent curdling. Serve hot with sour cream as a garnish.

Randy, our resident soup connoisseur, declared that this recipe tastes like a savory version of hot apple pie with whipped cream!

Cream of Green Apple Soup
8 servings

1/2 c.	yellow onion, finely chopped
1/2 c.	celery, finely chopped
4 c.	tart green apple, coarsely chopped
2 Tbsp.	canola or safflower oil
1/4 c.	unsalted butter
1/4 c.	unbleached flour
2 c.	milk, heated
1 tsp.	cinnamon
1/4 tsp.	nutmeg powder
2 tsp.	salt
1/4 tsp.	white pepper
2 c.	unfiltered apple juice
1/4 c.	sherry
1/2 c.	toasted pumpkin seeds for garnish, optional

Saute onion, celery and apples in oil until crisp-tender, about ten minutes. In a heavy-bottomed pot, make a roux by melting the butter, adding the flour and stirring together until smooth and bubbly (approximately seven minutes). Add the hot milk to the roux, whisking rapidly, until the sauce is smooth and creamy. Remove from the heat and keep warm. Add the remaining ingredients, except the seeds, to the sauteed apples and heat until hot. Stir in the cream sauce and blend well. Garnish with the toasted pumpkin seeds for extra texture.

Soup

Succotash Soup
8 servings

1 c.	dry white wine, chablis or fume blanc
4 c.	water or stock
2 c.	corn, frozen or canned will do, fresh is always best!
2 c.	fresh or frozen lima beans
1/2 c.	yellow onion, finely chopped
2	cloves garlic, minced
1/4 c.	unsalted butter
1/4 c.	unbleached flour
2 c.	milk, heated
1 tsp.	salt
1/4 tsp.	cracked pepper
1/4 tsp.	nutmeg powder
1/4 c.	fresh oregano, chopped (or 2 Tbsp. dried oregano)

Heat the corn, Lima beans and garlic gently in the water or stock and wine until hot and cooked through, approximately fifteen minutes. Make a white sauce (follow instruction in sherried cream of mushroom soup, page 76) and stir into the vegetables and broth with the salt, pepper and nutmeg. Garnish with oregano.

Creamy Turkey Garbanzo

4 c.	hummus (see recipe page 118)
6 c.	turkey stock
1 c.	turkey meat, finely chopped
1 c.	whole garbanzo beans, optional
1 tsp.	salt
1/2 tsp.	white pepper

Stir all ingredients together and heat until piping hot. Garnish with chopped parsley.

Cookery is not chemistry. It is an art. It requires instinct and taste rather than exact measurements. — X. Marcel Boulestin, etits et Grands Plats 1928

Bean soups are hearty and nourishing on wet winter days or anytime the mercury dips to parka-wearing levels. Country Fare's customers don't rely on the weather to favor this soup.

Turkey Black Bean
10 servings

4 c.	dry black beans, rinsed and picked over for stones
2	bay leaves
1/4 c.	olive oil
1/2 c.	yellow onion, finely chopped
4	cloves garlic, crushed
1	jalapeno pepper, minced
1 c.	bell pepper, finely chopped
1/2 c.	white wine
2 tsp.	salt
1/2 tsp.	white pepper
1/4 tsp.	cayenne pepper
4 c.	turkey or chicken stock
1 c.	cooked turkey meat, chopped
1/2 c.	fresh cilantro, minced

Cover the beans with water and soak overnight, or bring to a rolling boil, turn off heat, and let soak for one hour. Cook the beans with the bay leaves until tender, about one and one half hours, replenishing the water as it evaporates. Heat the olive oil and saute the vegetables about ten minutes. Add the wine and simmer for ten more minutes. Stir in the seasonings and one cup of the cooked beans. Puree the remaining beans with the turkey stock and add to the soup pot. Thin with more stock or water if necessary. Add the chopped turkey and cilantro, and heat until warmed through. Garnish with cilantro sour cream (see recipe page 212).

The first time I served this soup, it received a resounding cry of approval. The funny thing about it was that it was comprised of a conglomeration of leftover hors d'oeuvres which were prepared for the Thanksgiving holiday. Customers requested that I duplicate this soup, so I created this recipe using all of the best ingredients which make up stuffed mushrooms, twice-baked potatoes, and mornay sauce.

Turkey Stuffing Soup
12 servings

1/4 Tbsp.	unsalted butter
1/4 c.	unbleached flour
8 c.	turkey stock
1/2 c.	red onions, finely chopped
4	cloves garlic, crushed
1 Tbsp.	unsalted butter
4 c.	white mushrooms, baked for 15 minutes at 400 degrees, then finely chopped
8	small red potatoes, baked for 45 minutes at 400 degrees, then mashed with the skins
2 c.	turkey meat, chopped
1/2 c.	pecans, toasted and chopped
2 Tbsp.	tamari or soy sauce
2 Tbsp.	sherry
1/4 tsp.	white pepper
1/4 tsp.	nutmeg powder
2 c.	soft bread crumbs
1/4 c.	Parmesan cheese
1/4 c.	cheddar cheese, grated
1/2 c.	fresh herbs (any combination including basil, oregano parsley and sage), chopped

(continued)

Rational habits permit of discarding nothing left over, and the use to which leftovers...are put is often at the heart of a cooking's character. — Richard Olney

Soup

Make a roux by melting the butter, adding the flour, and cooking for five minutes, stirring constantly. Stir in 4 cups of the turkey stock and whisk quickly to form a thick veloute sauce. Remove from heat and keep hot. Saute the onions and garlic in the one tablespoon of additional butter until soft. Stir in the mushrooms, mashed potatoes, turkey, pecans and veloute sauce and add the remaining four cups turkey stock. Add the tamari, sherry, spices and bread crumbs. Dilute with a little water if too thick. Simmer for one half hour to soften all of the ingredients. Stir in the cheeses and blend well to melt into the hot soup. Add the herbs just before serving.

Navy Bean with Smoked Chicken
10 servings

1/2	smoked chicken, meat removed from bones and set aside
1 rib	celery
1 whole	carrot
1/2	medium yellow onion
2 whole	cloves garlic
6 sprigs	parsley
1/2 c.	sherry
8 c.	water
2	bay leaves
2 c.	small white navy beans, picked over for stones and washed
1 Tbsp.	canola or safflower oil
1/2 c.	celery, minced
1/2 c.	yellow onion, minced
1/2 c.	green bell peppers, finely chopped
1/2 c.	tomatoes, deseeded and chopped
4	cloves garlic, crushed
1 tsp.	salt
1/2 tsp.	cracked pepper

Cover the chicken bones, celery rib, carrot, half onion, garlic cloves and parsley sprigs with the water and sherry. Boil for one hour. Strain out the bones and refrigerate overnight. The fat will congeal on top of the stock and can be removed easily the following day. add the navy beans and bay leaves to the stock and cook vigorously for one and one half hours until beans are quite soft. Add water if the level of liquid reduces to below the top of the beans. Saute the chopped vegetables in the oil until crisp-tender, about ten minutes. Puree half of the cooked beans in a food processor or blender. Add the bean puree to the whole beans and stir in the cooked vegetables, salt and pepper. Add stock or water as desired to thin the soup. chop the reserved chicken meat and add to the soup, heating gently to prevent scorching. Serve hot with chopped cilantro to garnish.

Salads

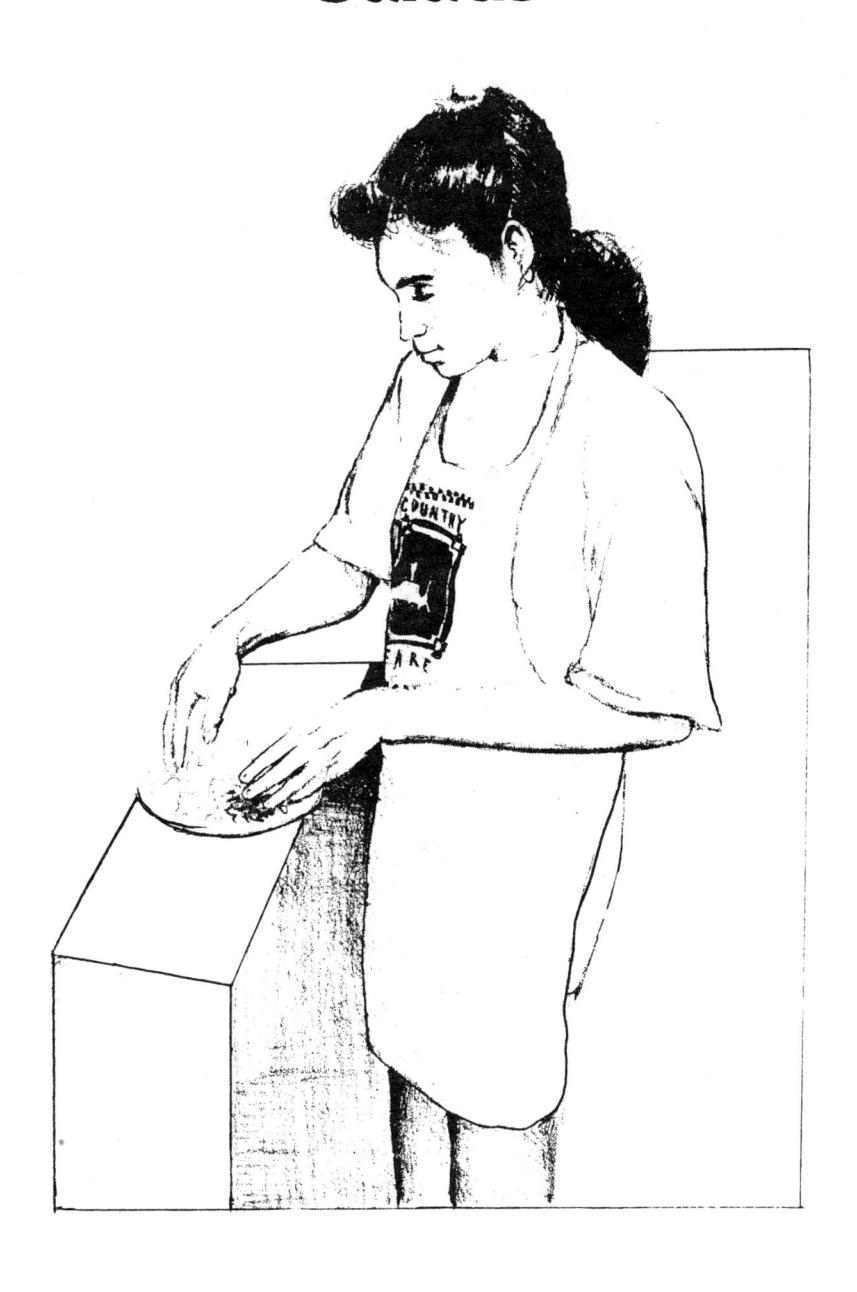

Aztec Black Bean 92
Buttermilk Coleslaw 93
Spicy Red Coleslaw 94
Carrot Salad with Honey-Yogurt Dressing 95
Tabbouli 96
Grandma C's Potato Salad 97
Couscous Salad 98
Greek Feta Salad 99
Russian Beet Salad 100
Savory Eggplant Salad 101
Pesto Pasta Salad 102
Pear, Cashew and Blue Cheese Salad 103
Russian Root Vegetable Salad 104
Orange Bean Salad 105
Curried Rice Salad 106
Sweet Potato Salad 107
Asian Rice Salad 108
Smoked Chicken Waldorf 109
Salad Olivier 110
Thai Chicken Salad 111
Garlic-Herb Dressing 112
Raspberry Vinaigrette 113

Salads

One of our most popular lunch items at Country Fare is the three salad sampler. As its name suggests, this salad plate consists of three customer-chosen scoops of the composed salads that we display in our deli case.

This section is filled with the recipes for all of the salads which we prepare for the hungry lunchtime masses. Most cooked vegetables are delicious tossed with a vinaigrette and chilled for salad use. The tart flavor of plain lowfat yogurt goes especially well with curries or fruit-based salads. We often use it as a reduced-fat substitute for mayonnaise or sour cream. Experiment with grains and vegetables in different combinations and add toasted nuts or seeds for added texture.

Aztec Black Bean
Serves 8

1 c.	red bell peppers, chopped
3 c.	black beans, cooked
1 1/2 c.	corn
1 c.	red onion, chopped
4	cloves garlic, chopped
1/2 c.	cilantro, chopped
1	jalapeno, minced
1/2 c.	olive oil
1/2 c.	lemon juice
1 tsp.	salt
1/4 tsp.	white pepper

Blend all of the salad ingredients together well and chill before serving.

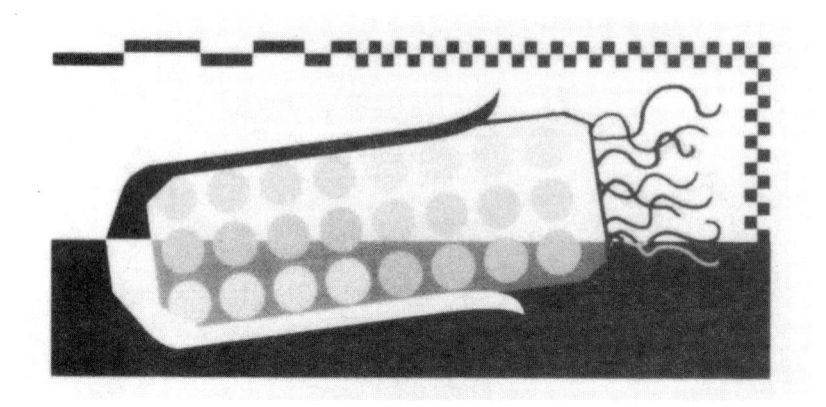

You are such an oasis on Fridays after a long week...signed, the teachers!

Salads

Buttermilk Coleslaw
Serves 6

6 c.	green cabbage, thinly shredded
1/4 c.	yellow onion, thinly sliced
1 c.	carrot, shredded
3/4 c.	mayonnaise
3/4 c.	buttermilk
1 tsp.	salt
2 Tbsp.	fresh dill, chopped

Mix all ingredients until thoroughly blended. Chill.

Spicy Red Coleslaw
Serves 6

6 c.	red cabbage, thinly shredded
1	egg
2 Tbsp.	honey mustard
3 Tbsp.	dijon mustard
3/4 c.	peanut oil
1 tsp.	salt
1/3 c.	wine vinegar
1/4 c.	plain yogurt
2 tsp.	celery seeds
2	cloves garlic, mashed
1/4 tsp.	white pepper

Blend the egg and mustards in a food processor. Slowly pour the oil in a thin stream and blend until thickened. Add the remaining ingredients and stir to combine. Toss this dressing with the red cabbage. Chill.

Our salad cook, Ana Salgado, makes almost 8 gallons of this crowd-pleaser each week to satisfy the tremendous customer demand!

Carrot Salad with Honey-Yogurt Dressing
Serves 8

6 c.	carrots, shredded and tossed with 1/4 c. orange juice
1 c.	raisins
1/2 c.	poppy seeds
1 c.	walnuts, toasted and chopped
2 c.	plain yogurt
1 c.	mayonnaise
1/2 c.	sour cream
1/2 c.	honey
1 tsp.	salt
1/4 tsp.	white pepper

Toss all ingredients together until thoroughly blended. Chill.

Peace. The sound of "The Planets" surrounds me, quietly heard from Cathy's "office." The light airy room holds its clientele well, saying to each: Welcome. The wonderful food served up with your name tempts the palette of the vegetarian or the rest of us. No greater place has chased the cares of the day and renewed my spirit. Thanks Cathy. — R.K.Bittencurt

Tabbouli

Serves 8

4 c.	bulgar
4 c.	boiling water
1/2 c.	mint, chopped
2 c.	parsley, chopped
2 c.	tomatoes, deseeded and chopped
2 c.	cucumber, peeled, deseeded and chopped
3	cloves garlic, mashed
1 c.	lemon juice
1 c.	olive oil
2 tsp.	salt
1/2 tsp.	cracked black pepper

Soak bulgar in the boiling water for 30 minutes. Mix in the chopped vegetables and dressing ingredients. Chill.

joe saxe

Grandma C's Potato Salad
serves 8

5 c.	new potatoes, quartered
1/2 c.	cider vinegar
1 c.	red onion , finely chopped
6	eggs, hard-boiled, peeled and chopped
1 tsp.	celery seed
2 tsp.	mustard seed
1 1/2 c.	mayonnaise
	salt and pepper to taste

Boil the potatoes for 30 minutes or until tender. Drain and sprinkle with the cider vinegar. Let cool. Combine the remaining ingredients and toss gently with the potatoes. Chill and keep cold before devouring.

Couscous Salad
Serves 6

2 c.	couscous
2 c.	boiling water
1/2 c.	red peppers, chopped
1/2 c.	zucchini, chopped
1/2 c.	carrots, grated
1/4 c.	green onions, sliced
1/2 c.	shelled pumpkin seeds, toasted
1/2 c.	garlic-herb dressing (see recipe page 112)

Pour the boiling water over the couscous and let stand until all of the water is absorbed, about ten minutes. Fluff the grains lightly, then stir in all of the remaining ingredients. Toss well to coat the ingredients well with the dressing. Chill.

Note: Don't overdress this salad or the tiny grains of couscous will stick together.

Greek Feta Salad
Serves 8

1 c.	fennel, thinly sliced
1 c.	celery, sliced diagonally
1 c.	cucumber, peeled, deseeded, and sliced
1 c.	tomatoes, deseeded and chopped (or use cherry tomatoes)
1 c.	feta cheese, crumbled
1/2 c.	onion, chopped
1/2 c.	garlic-herb dressing (see recipe page 112)

Mix all salad ingredients together carefully. Chill before serving.

The fennel is beyond every other vegetable, delicious. It greatly resembles in appearance the largest size celery, perfectly white, and there is no vegetable equals it in flavour. It is eaten at dessert, crude, and with, or without dry salt, indeed I prefer it to every other vegetable, or to any fruit. — Thomas Jefferson, Garden Book

Russian Beet Salad
Serves 8

4 c.	beets, cooked, peeled and cubed
2 c.	potatoes, cooked, peeled and cubed
1 c.	kosher pickles, chopped
1/2 c.	sour cream
1/2 c.	plain yogurt
1/4 c.	fresh dill, chopped

Blend yogurt, sour cream and dill together well. Stir in the remaining ingredients. Refrigerate overnight for the best flavor and visual appeal.

Savory Eggplant Salad
Serves 8

2 large	eggplants
1/2 c.	yellow onion, chopped
1/2 c.	red pepper, diced
1 c.	tomatoes, deseeded and chopped
1/2 c.	green onion, sliced
1/4 c.	parsley, chopped
4	cloves garlic, crushed
1/4 c.	tahini
1/4 c.	lemon juice
1/2 c.	olive oil
1 tsp.	salt
1/4 tsp.	cracked black pepper

Roast the whole unpeeled eggplants on a tray in a 400 degree oven for forty minutes. Cool, peel and chop the eggplant flesh into 1/2" cubes. Blend the dressing ingredients thoroughly until creamy and toss with the vegetables. Chill before serving.

Note: This salad makes a delicious vegetarian sandwich filling.

Some people's food always tastes better than others, even if they are cooking the same dish at the same dinner. Now I will tell you why--because one person has much more life in them--more fire, more vitality, more guts--than others. You have got to throw feeling into your cooking. — Rosa Lewis

Pesto Pasta Salad

Serves 8

Pesto Sauce

4 c.	fresh basil leaves
1/2 c.	toasted pinenuts
1 c.	olive oil
1/2 c.	grated Parmesan
6	cloves crushed garlic
1 tsp.	salt
1/2 tsp.	white pepper

Salad

6 c.	cooked pasta, chilled
1 c.	red pepper, chopped
1 c.	red onion, chopped
1/2 c.	celery, chopped
1/2 c.	black olives, sliced
1/2 c.	wine vinegar

Blend the pesto ingredients in a food processor until smooth. Toss with the remaining salad ingredients until thoroughly mixed.

Pear, Cashew and Blue Cheese Salad

Serves 8

8 large	ripe pears cut into 1/2 inch cubes
2 Tbsp.	lemon juice
2 c.	cashew pieces, toasted
1 1/2 c.	blue cheese, crumbled
1 c.	plain yogurt
1/4 c.	sour cream
1/4 c.	mayonnaise
1/2 c.	peanut oil
1/4 c.	cider vinegar
1/4 tsp.	white pepper
2 tsp.	honey
1 tsp.	salt

Toss the pear pieces gently in the lemon juice to prevent browning. Mix the dressing ingredients together and toss with the pears, cashews and blue cheese. Chill.

My friend Tatyana from St. Petersburg loves this salad. She makes it at home with whatever vegetables are available in season, although it must always contain beets and potatoes. The dressing is delicious for all types of marinated summertime vegetables.

Russian Root Vegetable Salad
Serves 8

1 lb.	russet potatoes, boiled, peeled and finely cubed
1 lb.	beets, boiled, peeled and finely cubed
1 large	kosher pickle, finely chopped
2	carrots, boiled, peeled and finely cubed
2	parsnips, boiled, peeled and finely cubed
1 knob	celery root, boiled, peeled and finely cubed
1 c.	yellow onion, finely chopped
1/2 c.	cider vinegar
1/4 c.	olive oil
4 tsp.	dijon mustard
4 tsp.	fructose or sugar
1/4 c.	water
2 tsp.	salt

Whisk together the vinegar, oil, mustard, fructose, water and salt. Cook the vegetables separately, or at the very least the beets and carrots, to prevent the color from bleeding into the white vegetables. Toss the cooked vegetables in the dressing while warm and then chill the salad before serving.

To make a good salad is to be a brilliant diplomatist-- the problem is entirely the same in both cases. To know how much oil one must mix with one's vinegar. — Oscar Wilde, Vera, or the Nihilists 1880

Orange Bean Salad
Serves 6

3/4 lb.	fresh green beans, sliced diagonally
1/2 c.	honey
1/4 c.	cider vinegar
1/2 c.	peanut oil
1/2 c.	orange juice
1/4 c.	cilantro, chopped
1/4 c.	parsley, chopped
1/2 c.	red onion, chopped
3	oranges, peeled and sectioned

Blanch the green beans in boiling water for five minutes. Drain and chill. Mix together the honey, vinegar, oil, juice, cilantro and parsley. Combine the beans, onions, orange sections and dressing. Chill.

Curried Rice Salad
Serves 8

6 c.	brown rice, cooked
2 Tbsp.	raisins
2 tsp.	diced jalapenos, deseeded
1/4 c.	red onion, chopped
2 Tbsp.	cilantro, chopped
2/3 c.	olive oil
1/3 c.	rice wine vinegar
	salt and pepper to taste
1/2 tsp.	dry mustard
2	cloves garlic, minced
1 Tbsp.	curry powder

Combine all ingredients and chill.

Salads

Sweet Potato Salad
8 servings

3 c.	sweet potatoes (about 3 medium), peeled and cut into 1/2 inch cubes
1 1/2 c.	purple potatoes (about 6 small), cut into 1/2 inch cubes
1 c.	pecans, toasted and coarsely chopped
1 c.	raspberry vinaigrette (see recipe page 113)

Cook sweet potatoes in boiling water for fifteen minutes or until tender. Drain well. Cook purple potatoes in boiling water in a separate pot for ten minutes or until tender. Drain well. Toss with raspberry vinaigrette and the chopped pecans.

I was required by a catering client to make a luncheon side dish for a group of visiting Japanese businessmen. This recipe was a big hit!

Asian Rice Salad
Serves 6

3 c.	brown rice, cooked
1 c.	carrots, peeled and shredded
1/2 c.	green onions, sliced
1/2 c.	sesame seeds, toasted
1/2 c.	mushrooms, sliced
1/2 c.	mung bean sprouts
1/4 c.	sesame oil
1/4 c.	tamari or soy sauce
3	cloves garlic, mashed
1 tsp.	fresh ginger, grated
1/4 c.	rice wine vinegar
1/4 tsp.	white pepper

Whisk together the oil, tamari, garlic, ginger, vinegar and pepper. Toss this dressing with the rice, vegetables and sesame seeds. Chill before serving. This salad is also delicious served at room temperature or heated gently as a side dish for grilled teriyaki chicken, fish, tempeh or tofu.

Salads

Smoked Chicken Waldorf
serves 6

- 3 c.   smoked chicken, chopped
- 3 c.   celery, sliced
- 2 c.   walnuts, toasted and chopped
- 4 c.   tart apples, chopped
- 1 c.   mayonnaise
- 1/2 c.   plain lowfat yogurt

Mix all ingredients together and refrigerate. Serve chilled.

Note: Try smoked chicken waldorf salad on pumpernickel bread for an unusual sandwich. It makes an elegant canape on cocktail-sized bread or tiny croissants.

Salad Olivier
serves 8

1 lb.	smoked chicken meat
1 lb.	russett potatoes, peeled
1	large kosher pickle
1 c.	green peas
1	tart apple, peeled
1 c.	yellow onion, finely chopped
1 Tbsp.	dill, minced
1/2 c.	mayonnaise
1/4 c.	sour cream
2	eggs, hard-cooked, peeled, and finely chopped

Cut potatoes into 1/2 inch cubes and boil for 15 minutes. Drain well and chill. Cube smoked chicken, pickle, and apple and toss with the potatoes, onion and peas. Blend the mayonnaise, sour cream and dill and gently fold in the cubed vegetables and chicken. Chill well. Serve garnished with the hard-cooked egg.

Note: Salad olivier is a classic appetizer on the Russian *zakuski* (hors d'oeuvres) table. Serve with dark bread.

Thai Chicken Salad
Serves 6

2 c.	snow peas, blanched in hot water for two minutes, drained and chilled
2 c.	fresh mung bean sprouts
2 c.	mushrooms, sliced
1/2 c.	red pepper, chopped
1/2 c.	carrots, peeled and shredded
2 c.	cooked chicken, chopped
1 c.	spicy peanut sauce (see recipe page 208)
1/2 c.	plain lowfat yogurt
1/2 c.	mayonnaise

Blend the peanut sauce well with the yogurt and mayonnaise. Carefully toss the vegetables and chicken with this dressing. Chill well before serving. Garnish with sliced green onion and toasted peanuts.

Just climbed out of the Grand Canyon yesterday. I am sore, this is the first food I get to eat. I hope it's... Yep!!
— Rob 8/21/89

Garlic-Herb Dressing

Makes 1 quart

1/2 c.	lemon juice
1 c.	white wine or champagne vinegar
2 c.	olive oil
1 tsp.	salt
4	cloves garlic, mashed
1/2 tsp.	white pepper
1/2 tsp.	dry mustard
1 tsp.	fresh basil, chopped
1/2 tsp.	fresh oregano, chopped
1/2 tsp.	fresh thyme, chopped
1/2 tsp.	fresh sage, chopped
1/2 tsp.	fresh lovage or celery leaves, chopped

Blend all ingredients well in a food processor or blender. Chill well.

Raspberry Vinaigrette
makes 1 pint

1/2 c.	raspberry vinegar
1/2 c.	canola or safflower oil
1/2 c.	olive oil
2 Tbsp.	dijon mustard
1/4 c.	brown sugar
1/4 tsp.	salt
2 tsp.	garlic, mashed
2 Tbsp.	shallots, finely minced (or substitute 1 Tbsp. red onion)
2 tsp.	fresh mint, chopped

Blend all of the ingredients well and refrigerate.

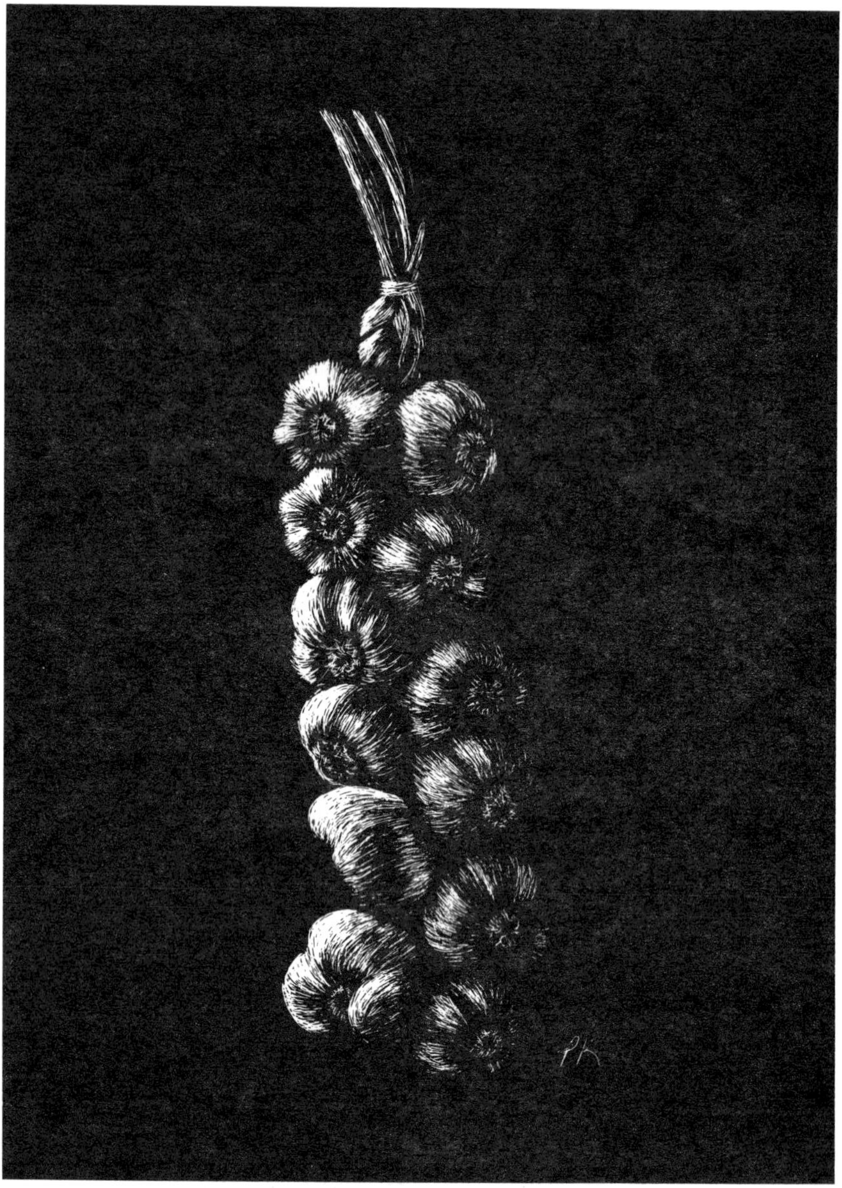

Sandwiches & "Fist Food"

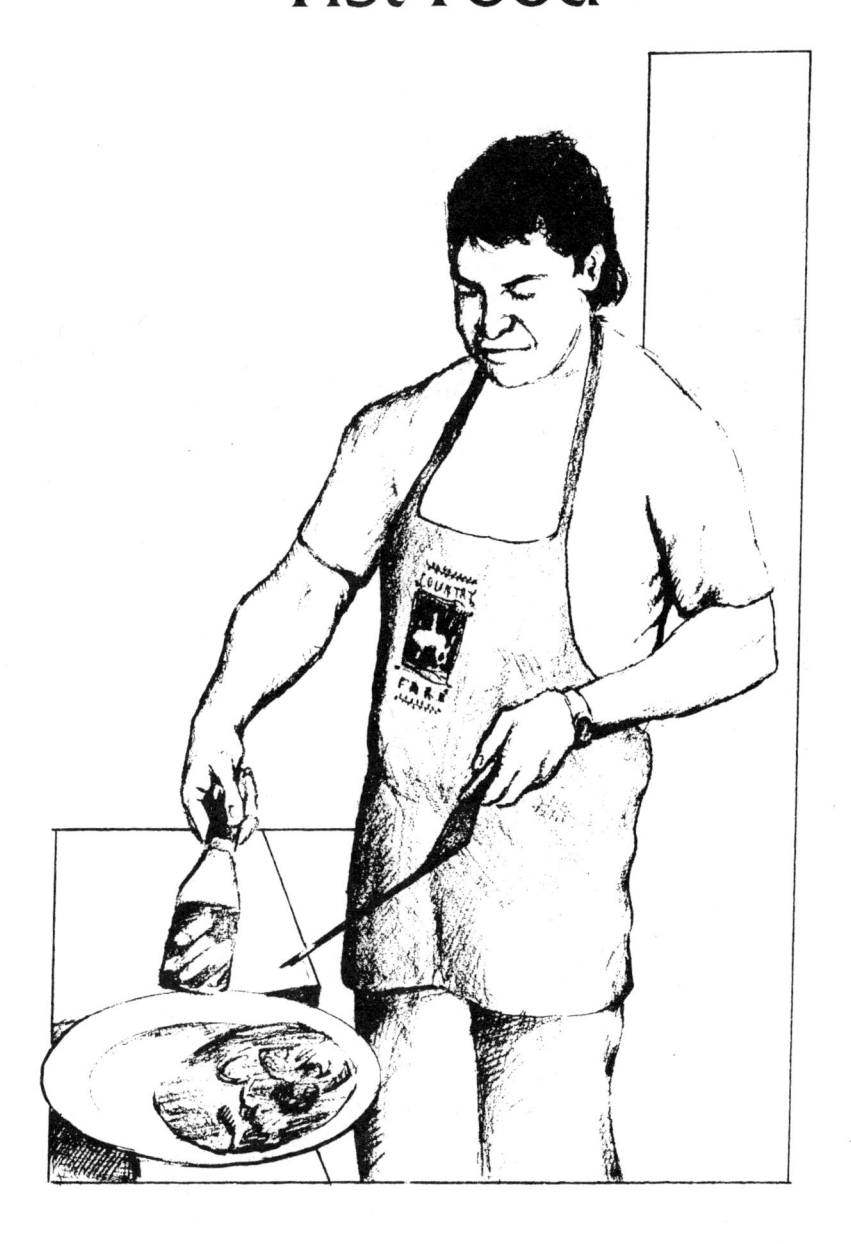

Hummus 118
Tuna Salad 119
Egg and Olive Salad 120
Hard-Boiled Eggs 121
Chicken Salad with Toasted Almonds 122
Seafood Salad 123
Salmon Salad with Capers and Dill 124
Cinnamon-Brandied Apples 125
Empanadas 126
Piroshki Short Dough 128
Yeasted Piroshki Dough 130
Vegetarian Fajitas 131
Grilled Breast of Chicken 132
Turkey Burger 134
Veggie Burger 135
Falafel Patties 136
Turkey Sausage 137
Turkey Sausage Meatball Sandwich 138
Spanakopita 139
Sausage and Spinach Stuffed Brioche 140

Sandwiches & "Fist Food"

The most obvious choice for lunch in an American restaurant is the ubiquitous sandwich. We use only free-range turkey from Diestel Turkey Ranch, a small family farm in Sonora, California. Joan Diestel also produces our nitrate-free smoked turkey breasts which we use in sandwiches and in a variety of salads which would normally contain ham. Smoked turkey is much lower in fat than ham, but has a similar flavor and texture. By far, the favorite hand-held lunch is either a grilled sandwich such as the eggplant sandwich or any of the self-contained meals which I call "fist food." These items are dough-wrapped lunches like empanadas, spanakopitas, piroshki or burritos. "Fist food" travels well and can often be eaten on the run. The fillings have endless possibilities, and I recommend trying various combinations to create custom-made favorites.

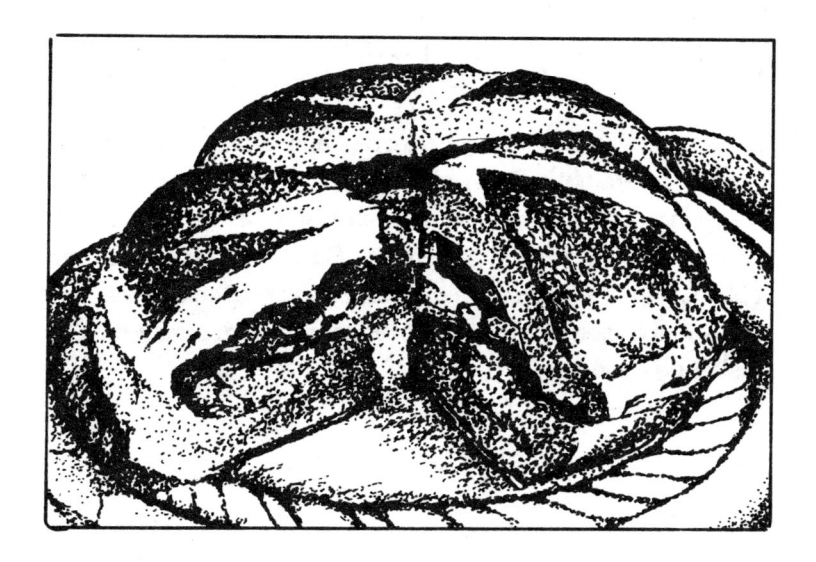

Chill hummus to use in vegetarian sandwiches with lots of veggies and a thin spread of toasted sesame tahini. You can also blend hummus half and half with plain yogurt for a tasty dip with crackers, pita bread triangles or raw vegetables.

Hummus
Serves 8

4 c.	cooked garbanzo beans (see note below) or two 16 — ounce cans precooked garbanzo beans
3/4 c.	tahini
4	cloves garlic, mashed
1/2 c.	lemon juice
1 1/2 tsp.	salt
1/4 c.	parsley, chopped
1/4 tsp.	cracked black pepper

Puree the garbanzo beans and garlic in a food processor or blender gradually adding the liquid that they are cooked or canned in to create a thick puree. Blend in the tahini, lemon juice, salt, pepper and parsley.

Note: To cook dry garbanzo beans, soak 2 cups of beans in water overnight. Drain off the soaking water and cover the beans in a pot with 6 cups of fresh water. Bring to a boil and then turn the heat down to medium. Cook the beans for 3 hours, replenishing the water as it evaporates. Cooking garbanzo beans is a tedious process. Using canned beans may be a less frustrating option.

Sandwiches & "Fist Food"

Country Fare uses only line-caught albacore tuna which is fresh-frozen on the fishing boat. The taste is delicate, and sometimes puzzled customers think it is chicken salad.

Tuna Salad
Serves 6

4 c.	canned or poached fresh tuna, drained
1 c.	chopped celery
1/2 c.	grated yellow onion
1/4 tsp.	white pepper
3/4 c.	mayonnaise
1/2 c.	plain yogurt

Finely chop the cooked tuna, Stir in the remaining ingredients and chill before serving.

Egg and Olive Salad
Serves 6

1 dozen	hard-boiled eggs, peeled
1/2 c.	celery, chopped
1/2 c.	green olives, sliced
1/2 c.	mayonnaise
2 Tbsp.	sour cream
1/2 tsp.	salt
1/8 tsp.	white pepper
pinch	cayenne pepper

Coarsely chop the peeled eggs. Combine all of the other ingredients and blend gently with the eggs. Chill.

Hard-Boiled Eggs

Place room temperature eggs in a saucepan with a loose-fitting lid to allow some of the steam to escape. Cover the eggs with tepid water and place the saucepan over a medium high heat. Set the timer for 17 minutes. When the water boils rapidly, turn the heat down to simmer and keep the saucepan covered. When the timer sounds, drain the eggs and plunge them into an ice water bath to stop the cooking. Crack the shells to allow water to seep under for easier peeling, and then allow the eggs to cool. Peel them immediately and chill before using or refrigerate in the shells to store for up to one week. If storing without the protective shells, submerge the cooked eggs in cold water to cover. Peeled eggs keep for four to five days at most. Interesting tip: really fresh eggs are harder to peel when boiled. Use eggs that are several days old.

There is always a best way of doing everything, if it be to be to boil an egg. — Ralph Waldo Emerson

Our Oriental chicken salad is a favorite with the "regulars." We serve it on a huge nest of fried rice stick noodles nestled on a bed of fresh organic lettuces. Surround the mound of chicken salad with garden-fresh raw vegetables and sprinkle the toasted almonds liberally on top.

Chicken Salad with Toasted Almonds
Serves 6

4 c.	cooked chicken meat, chopped into 1/2 inch cubes
1/2 c.	chopped red onions
1 c.	chopped celery
1 c.	sliced water chestnuts
1 c.	chopped red peppers or pimentos
1 c.	mayonnaise
1 c.	plain yogurt
1/4 c.	dry sherry
1/2 c.	toasted slivered almonds

Blend all salad ingredients together and chill well before serving.

Variation: Substitute toasted cashews or peanuts for the almonds.

Sandwiches & "Fist Food"

Seafood Salad
Serves 6

1 1/2 c.	poached bay shrimp (if using prawns, chop into 1/2 inch pieces)
1 1/2 c.	poached bay scallops (if using sea scallops, chop into 1/2 inch pieces)
1 1/2 c.	Dungeness crabmeat
1/2 c.	green onions, sliced
1 c.	celery, sliced
1 c.	jicama, peeled and chopped
1 c.	mayonnaise
2 Tbsp.	lemon juice

Blend all salad ingredients together and chill before serving.

joe saxe

Salmon Salad with Capers and Dill

Serves 6

4 c.	canned or freshly poached salmon, bones and skin removed
1 c.	red onion, chopped
1/2 c.	capers
1/2 c.	fresh dill, chopped
1 c.	mayonnaise
2 Tbsp.	lemon juice

Blend all salad ingredients together and chill before serving.

This is the best place to have a good lunch, especially when one is in a hurry. I can't think of another spot to get quality sandwiches and friendly service. It's like eating in your own kitchen, except you don't have to do anything but sit and chew. Great place! — Nona

Sandwiches & "Fist Food"

We serve cinnamon-brandied apples on a sandwich with cream cheese and roasted cashew butter. One of our favorite regulars, Lori, varies her sandwich by substituting cheddar cheese for the cream cheese. Pair these crisp-tender flavorful apples with peanut butter or almond butter for another variation on the theme.

Cinnamon-Brandied Apples
Serves 6

6	large apples, cored, peeled, and sliced
2 Tbsp.	unsalted butter
1/4 c.	brown sugar
1 1/2 tsp.	cinnamon
1/4 c.	Calvados or brandy

Saute the apple slices in the butter until soft. Stir in the brown sugar and the cinnamon. Add the brandy and cook until the flame from the alcohol subsides. Chill before serving.

The discovery of a new dish does more for human happiness than the discovery of a new star. — Jean-Anthelme Brillat-Savarin, La Physiologie du Gout 1825

Empanadas

serves 6

3 c.	unbleached flour
1 tsp.	baking powder
2 tsp.	coriander powder
1/2 lb.	unsalted butter, grated
1/2 lb.	cream cheese
1/2 tsp.	cider vinegar
4 tsp.	water
1/4 c.	olive oil
1/2 c.	broccoli, chopped
1/2 c.	green pepper, chopped
1/2 c.	red pepper, chopped
1/2 c.	carrots, chopped
1/2 c.	cauliflower, chopped
1/2 c.	zucchini squash, chopped
1 c.	jack cheese, grated
1/2 c.	olives, chopped
2	jalapeno peppers, deseeded and chopped

To prepare the dough:

Combine the first three dry ingredients together. Blend the butter and the cream cheese into the dry ingredients. Add the vinegar and the water and bring together into a soft dough.

To prepare the filling:

Saute the vegetables in the olive oil. Stir in the cheese, olives and jalapenos.

Everybody, This is the only health food restaurant that has GREAT food. I come here all the time with my mom, and we love it. Keep up the good work. — Michelle October 2, 1991

To assemble the empanadas:

Divide the dough into 3 ounce balls. Roll each ball into a 6 inch circle on a floured board. Place 1/2 c.
of the filling on one half of the dough circle and fold the pastry over the filling to form a half moon. Crimp the edge well with a fork and brush the surface with an egg wash (one egg beaten with one tablespoon of water). Bake at 400 degrees for 20 minutes or until golden brown.

Piroshkis are the mainstay of a well-laden *zakuski* or Russian hors d'oeuvres table. They are delicious small bites combined with the traditional salty and rich appetizers of this favorite Russian meal. I love piroshki in place of bread with borscht or with other hearty soups.

Piroshki Short Dough
makes enough for 2 dozen small piroshki

4 c.	all-purpose flour
1/2 c.	unsalted butter, softened
1/2 c.	sour cream
1/2 tsp.	salt
2 tsp.	baking powder

Blend the flour, salt, and baking powder together. Combine with the butter and sour cream to form a soft dough. Chill until ready to use.

Piroshki Filling

1/4 c.	unsalted butter
4 c.	green cabbage, finely shredded
2 c.	leeks, washed well and thinly sliced
4 c.	mushrooms, sliced
1/2 c.	fresh dill, chopped
3	eggs, hard-cooked
1 tsp.	salt
1/4 tsp.	white pepper

Saute the cabbage, leeks, and mushrooms in the butter. Allow to cool. Stir in the dill, chopped eggs, salt, and pepper to the cooled vegetables.

Roll out the dough and cut with a large round cookie cutter or a wide-mouthed glass. Place 2 tablespoons of the vegetable mixture on half of the dough and fold the unfilled side over the filling. Seal with an egg wash and crimp the edges with a fork dipped in flour. Brush egg wash over the entire surface and bake at 400 degrees for 15 minutes.

Egg Wash

For shiny crusts on baked pies, pastries and breads, an egg wash creates the best glossy finish. Simply beat an egg with a tablespoon of water until foamy. To reduce the cholesterol, use only the egg white and water. Brush the egg wash on the pastry lightly with a pastry brush to coat thinly and evenly.

Note: This is a quick version of Russian piroshki which I use for hors d'oeuvres. Try the yeast dough (recipe follows) for a heartier version to serve for lunch with borscht.

Yeasted Piroshki Dough
serves 8

1 c.	milk, warmed to room temperature
1 1/2 Tbsp.	yeast
1 Tbsp.	fructose or sugar
3 c.	unbleached flour
2	eggs, beaten
1/4 c.	unsalted butter, melted

Sprinkle the yeast and fructose over the warm milk. Stir well, then set near the stove or another warm place until the mixture foams, about 5 minutes. Stir in the flour, eggs and butter and knead as for bread dough for 10 minutes. Add more flour if necessary. Put in clean bowl, cover with plastic wrap and set near the stove to rise for 40 minutes.

Portion the dough into 8 balls. Roll each ball carefully on a floured board to form a circle approximately 6 inches in diameter. Place 1/2 cup of the vegetable mixture in the center of each circle and fold two edges in, overlapping to seal. Pinch well. Fold the other two edges over and pinch well to seal. Turn the piroshki smooth side up and brush lightly with an egg wash. Bake at 400 degrees for 20 to 25 minutes or until puffed and golden brown.

Note: This dough is much more laborious to prepare, but it does result in an authentic Russian piroshki. Normally this dough is fried in hot oil, but I suggest baking it for a lower fat result.

Vegetarian Fajitas
serves 4

Spice Mixture:
1 Tbsp.	granulated garlic
1 tsp.	cumin
2 tsp.	salt
1 tsp.	paprika
1/4 tsp.	white pepper
1/4 tsp.	cayenne pepper

Stir the ingredients together well and store in a shaker in a cool dry place.

2 Tbsp.	olive oil
1 Tbsp.	lime or lemon juice
1 lb.	tempeh, cut in thin strips
2 c.	bell peppers, cut in thin strips
2 c.	red onions, thinly sliced
8 large	whole wheat or flour tortillas
1 c.	cilantro sour cream (see recipe page 212)
1 c.	salsa fresca (see recipe page 203)

Toss the tempeh, peppers and onions with the lime or lemon juice and sprinkle with 1 Tbsp. of the spice mixture. Fry the tempeh and vegetables in olive oil until crisp tender, about 5 minutes. Steam the tortillas in a Chinese bamboo steamer or sprinkle lightly with water and steam in a microwave oven for 30 seconds on high. Serve the tortillas with the tempeh mixture, the cilantro sour cream and salsa fresca on the side.

Inhabitants of underdeveloped nations and victims of natural disasters are the only people who have ever been happy to see soybeans. — Fran Lebowitz, Metropolitan Life 1978

Grilled Breast of Chicken
Serves 6

Red Pepper Rouille Sauce

1 c.	bread crumbs
1/2 c.	water
4	canned pimentos (or 4 roasted, skinned, seeded red peppers)
2 tsp.	red pepper flakes
8	cloves garlic
1 c.	olive oil
4 Tbsp.	chicken stock
1 tsp.	salt

Marinade for Chicken

6	boneless skinless chicken 1/2 breasts
1/2	c. lemon juice
3/4 c.	olive oil
2 tsp	garlic, minced
4 tsp	onion, minced
	salt and pepper to taste
1 Tbsp.	fresh thyme, chopped

Soak the bread crumbs in water. Puree the pimentos, bread crumbs, pepper flakes and garlic in a food processor until smooth. Slowly add the oil as in making mayonnaise. Stir in chicken stock to thin the sauce. Add salt to taste.

Whisk the marinade ingredients together and marinate the chicken breasts 1 hour or more before grilling.

(continued)

Assembly

  2   large eggplants, peeled
  6   crusty sourdough rolls

Cut the eggplant into 1/2" thick slices. Place on an olive oiled baking sheet and sprinkle with salt. Roast 15 minutes until soft. Spread the bottom slice of a crusty roll generously with red pepper rouille and place a grilled chicken breast on top. Top the chicken with two roasted eggplant slices and 2 ounces of fontina cheese. Melt the cheese under a broiler or in a microwave oven and top the sandwich with bread that has been spread with butter or mayonnaise.

Turkey Burger

makes 4 large burgers

1 lb.	ground turkey
1 c.	bread crumbs
1	egg, beaten
1/2 c.	yellow onions, pureed
1/4 c.	Italian parsley, chopped
1 tsp.	salt
1/4 tsp.	white pepper

Blend all of the ingredients together well. Shape into 4 large burgers. Grill or fry on both sides for approximately four minutes per side.

Note: Turkey burger mix also can be shaped into meatballs. Fry them in canola oil until browned, drain and then finish cooking in a 350 degree oven for approximately 30 minutes.

Pepper is small in quantity and great in virtue. — Plato, Laws 360 BC

Veggie Burger
Makes 12 six ounce burgers

3 c.	sweet potatoes, cooked and mashed
1 c.	green onions or leeks, sliced
4 c.	cooked brown rice (or millet, quinoa or similar grain)
1 c.	walnuts, chopped
2 c.	cheddar cheese, grated
2 c.	bread crumbs
1	egg, beaten
2 tsp.	salt
1/4 tsp.	white pepper
1/2 c.	parsley, chopped
1/2 c.	sesame seeds, toasted

Mix together all of the ingredients and form into 6 ounce patties. Fry on a hot oiled griddle for approximately four minutes. Flip the burgers, and then cover them with a pot lid while cooking the second side to steam-cook them.

There is no disease, bodily or mental, which adoption of vegetable diet, and pure water has not infallibly mitigated, wherever the experiment has been fairly tried.
— Percy Bysshe Shelley, Queen Mab 1813

Falafel Patties
serves 4

4 c.	hummus (see recipe page 118)
1/4 tsp.	tumeric powder
1/4 tsp.	cumin, ground
1/8 tsp.	cayenne powder
1	egg, beaten
1/2 c.	bread crumbs
3/4 c.	unbleached flour
1/2 c.	canola or safflower oil, heated

Mix all of the ingredients together. Shape into 2 ounce patties and dust with flour. Fry in hot oil until brown on both sides. Serve in warmed pita bread drizzled with tahini sauce (see recipe page 159) and with tabbouli salad as a side dish (see recipe page 96).

Sandwiches & "Fist Food"

Turkey Sausage

2 lbs.	ground turkey
2 tsp.	fennel seed or powder
1/2 tsp.	crushed red chilies
2 tsp.	salt
1/4 tsp.	black pepper
1 tsp.	cumin powder
1/4 tsp.	nutmeg powder
6 cloves	crushed garlic

Blend all ingredients together well and refrigerate.

Salt is born of the purest of parents: the sun and the sea. — Pythagoras

Turkey Sausage Meatball Sandwich
serves 2

1/2 lb.	turkey sausage (see recipe previous page)
2 Tbsp.	olive oil
1 c.	bell peppers, thinly sliced
1 c.	red onions, thinly sliced
1 c.	marinara sauce (see recipe page 206)
1/2 c.	mozzarella or provolone cheese, grated
1/4 c.	Parmesan cheese
2	crusty French rolls

Preheat the oven to 350 degrees. Cut the turkey sausage into 8 portions and roll the pieces into 8 balls. Fry the meatballs in the olive oil over a medium heat until browned. Remove the meatballs from the oil and transfer them to a baking dish. Finish cooking the meatballs in a 350 degree oven for 30 minutes. Fry the peppers and onions in the leftover oil and drain well. Heat the sauce over a medium heat or in a microwave oven. To assemble the sandwich: Cut the rolls in half crosswise and pull out the soft interior bread. Place the meatballs and sauteed vegetables in the bottom halves of the rolls. Pour the sauce over each and sprinkle with the cheeses. Heat under a broiler to melt the cheese, and then replace the top crusts. Cut in half and serve with lots of napkins.

America is a confirmed sandwich nation. Everywhere you go you find sandwich stands, sandwich shops, and nine out of ten people seem to stick to the sandwich-and-a-glass-of-milk or cup-of-coffee luncheon. — James Beard

Spanakopita
Serves 8

8 c.	raw spinach, washed well, steamed, drained and chopped
6	eggs, beaten
1/2 c.	unbleached flour
1/2 c.	Parmesan cheese
1 c.	crumbled feta cheese
1/2 c.	ricotta cheese
1/4 tsp.	nutmeg
1/4 tsp.	white pepper

Blend all of the ingredients together in a food processor. Butter and stack three layers of phyllo dough and fold it in half lengthwise. Place a 3 ounce spoonful of the filling on the top right corner of the short end of this long column of buttered phyllo dough. Fold the filling and dough down towards the left edge to form a triangular pocket. Bring this fat triangle of dough and filling straight down over the buttered phyllo, matching the edges in a straight line. Continue folding the dough and encased filling evenly, keeping the edges of the column straight. The final package will look like a neatly folded flag. Butter the top surface well and place on a parchment paper-lined baking sheet. Bake at 400 degrees for 20 minutes or until brown.

Note: Mini spanakopitas are an enticing hors d'oeuvre at buffet parties. Cut three sheets of buttered phyllo dough in four parallel strips and place a tablespoon of filling at the top of each strip. Fold the dough as instructed in the recipe and bake as indicated.

Sausage and Spinach Stuffed Brioche
serves 6

Filling

2 lb.	turkey sausage (see recipe page 137)
1 c.	yellow onion, finely chopped
3	cloves garlic, crushed
4 c.	fresh spinach, chopped
1/4 tsp.	black pepper
1/2 tsp.	salt
1 tsp.	fresh thyme
1/4 tsp.	Tabasco sauce
2	eggs, beaten
6	eggs, hard-cooked and peeled

Brown the sausage well. Remove from the pan and crumble into small pieces. Cook the onion, garlic and spinach in the turkey sausage drippings. Add the spices and simmer for five minutes. Blend the meat and vegetables together and allow to cool. Stir in the beaten eggs.

Brioche Dough

1/2 c.	milk, heated until lukewarm
1/2 c.	cold unsalted butter, cut into small pieces
6 Tbsp.	fructose or sugar
1/2 tsp.	salt
2 Tbsp.	yeast
1/2 c.	warm water
4 1/2 c.	unbleached flour
4	eggs

(continued)

Stir the butter into the warm milk. Add the fructose and salt and cool to room temperature. Soften the yeast in the warm water. Stir in the milk mixture and two cups of the flour. Beat well. Add the eggs and two to two and one half cups of the flour to make a thick batter. Beat in a mixer with a dough hook for approximately five minutes or with a wooden spoon for fifteen minutes. Cover the dough with plastic and let rise until doubled in volume, about one hour. Stir dough down and set aside.

Assembly

Cut the dough into two balls. Press one ball into a glass pie plate, pressing evenly up the sides to form a crust. Fill the crust with 1/2 of the sausage/spinach mixture. Press the peeled hard-cooked eggs in a ring around the center. Fill with the remaining sausage/spinach mixture. Top with the remaining dough and let rise until almost doubled in size, about thirty minutes. Brush with the beaten egg and bake at 400 degrees for twenty-five minutes. Cover with foil and bake an additional fifteen minutes. Cut into six wedges and serve immediately.

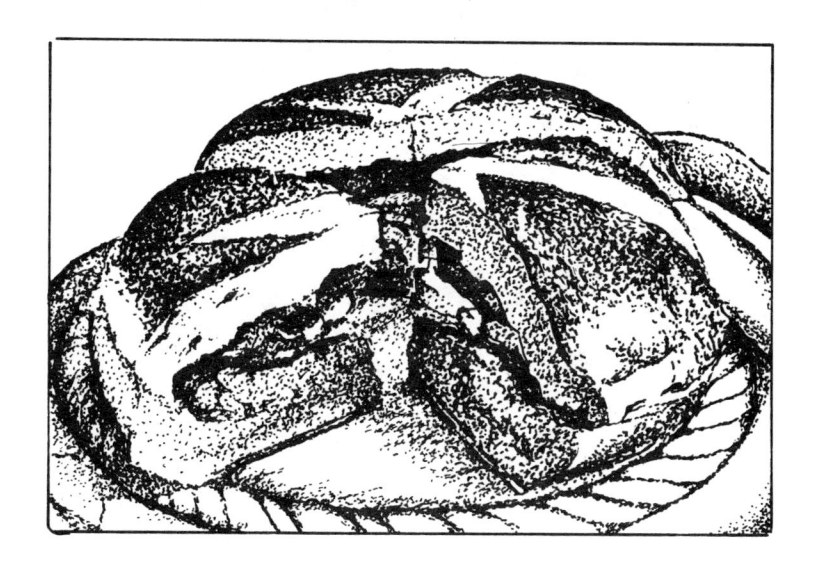

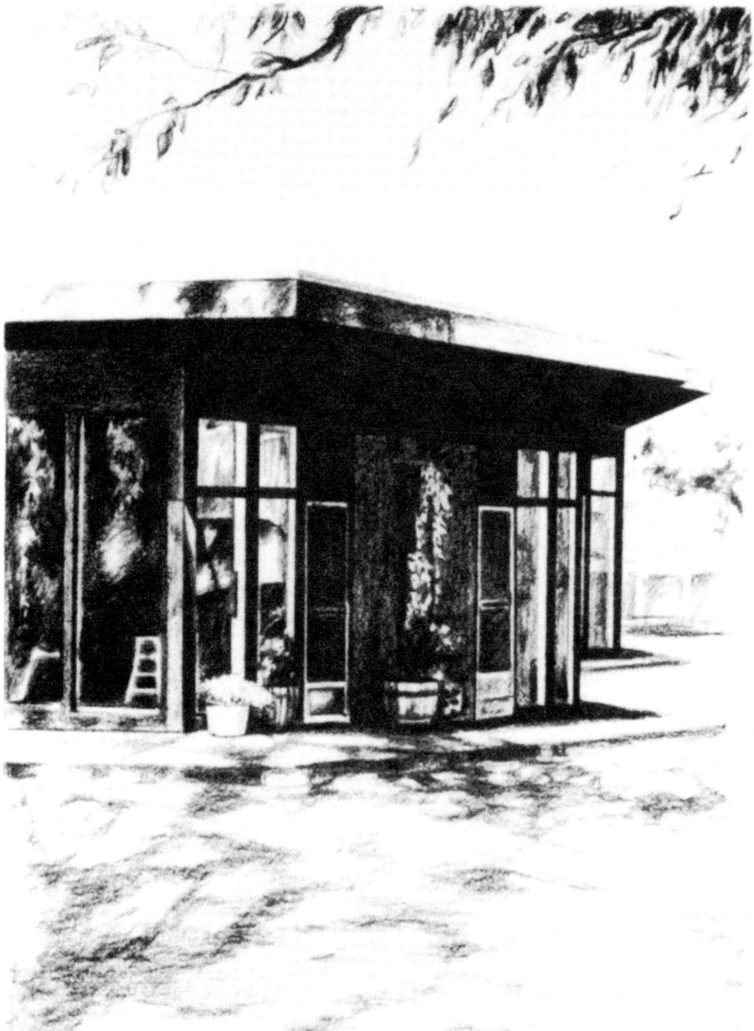

Appetizers

Stuffed Mushrooms with Fresh Herbs 146
Stuffed Eggs Russian-Style 147
Vegetarian Spring Rolls 148
Eggplant Caviar 149
Dolmas 150
Pecan Baked Chicken Drumettes 151
Teriyaki Tofu 152
Smoked Tuna Mousse 153
Yogurt Cheese 154
Boursin 155
Boursin Dip 156
Dijon Dip 157
Tapenade 158
Tahini Sauce 159
Roasted Garlic Spread 160
Roasted Red Pepper Spread 161
Guacamole 162

Appetizers

Appetizers are the most pleasing little nibbles available for parties of any magnitude. Country Fare caters a variety of events, and most customers delight in having one or two hors d'oeuvres in addition to their meals. We have prepared countless wedding buffets consisting of a dozen or so appetizers only! Paired with a fine champagne or sparkling apple cider, hors d'oeuvres alone can suffice as an elegant repast.

There are numerous ways to create suitable dishes for the appetizer course of a meal with recipes found throughout this book.. Potato pancakes can be prepared as small as silver dollars and served with cranberry catsup, red onion marmalade or mango chutney. A fresh fruit platter is more festive when served with a bowl of honey yogurt sauce. Grilled or poached prawns are delicious when served with a dipping sauce — try mango chutney, pesto or orange-tamari sauce. A pleasing holiday appetizer can be prepared by wrapping a whole small brie (or similar soft cheese with a rind) in brioche, phyllo or puff pastry dough. Wrap the pastry carefully around the cheese and place on a parchment paper-lined baking sheet. Brush brioche or puff pastry doughs with an egg wash for a shiny crust. Bake at 400 degrees until golden brown, approximately 30 minutes. Serve with sliced baguettes and crackers.

Stuffed Mushrooms with Fresh Herbs

Serves 6

30	mushrooms, wiped clean with a towel, reserve stems
4 Tbsp.	clarified butter or olive oil
1/2 c.	yellow onions, finely chopped
2	cloves garlic, minced
1/4 c.	fresh basil or oregano, chopped
1/2 tsp.	salt
1/4 tsp.	white pepper
1/2 c.	Parmesan cheese
1 c.	bread crumbs
1 c.	cheddar cheese, grated

Preheat the oven to 375 degrees. Chop the mushroom stems finely. Saute the chopped stems with the chopped onion and garlic in the clarified butter for fifteen minutes, stirring often. Mix in the remaining ingredients. Stuff the mushroom caps with this mixture. Place the mushroom caps on a parchment paper-lined baking tray and bake at 375 degrees for twenty-five minutes.

Life is too short to stuff a mushroom. — Shirley Conran

Appetizers

Stuffed Eggs Russian-Style
serves 8

1/4 c.	butter, melted
1/4 c.	yellow onion, finely chopped
2 c.	mushrooms, thinly sliced
1/2 c.	sour cream or plain yogurt
2 tsp.	dijon mustard
8	eggs, hard-cooked, peeled and cut in 1/2 lengthwise
1/4 c.	parsley, chopped
1/4 c.	dill, chopped
2 Tbsp.	mayonnaise
1/2 tsp.	salt
1/4 tsp.	pepper

Saute the onion and mushrooms in the melted butter. Stir in the sour cream and mustard and cook over high heat for 5 minutes. Cool. Mash the yolks with the cooled vegetable mixture. Add the herbs, mayonnaise, salt and pepper and mix thoroughly. Mound the yolk mixture in the egg white halves with a spoon or pipe the filling back into the egg whites with a pastry bag fitted with a star tip.

Vegetarian Spring Rolls
serves 8

1/2 c.	bean sprouts
1 c.	green cabbage, shredded
1/2 c.	broccoli, chopped
1/2 c.	yellow onion, chopped
1/2 c.	celery , sliced
1/2 c.	carrot, grated
2 Tbsp.	peanut oil
1/2 c.	cashews, toasted and chopped
1/2 c.	tofu, finely cubed
2	cloves garlic, minced
1 tsp.	salt
1 pkg.	egg roll wrappers
	peanut oil for frying

Stir-fry the vegetables in the 2 Tbsp. peanut oil. Add the cashews, tofu, garlic and salt. Fill each egg roll wrapper with 1/4 cup filling and roll like a cigar, folding the sides in after the first turn and rolling tightly to form a neat cylinder. Dab the inside of the final flap with a little water to create a tight seal.. Fill a steep-sided skillet one inch deep with peanut oil and heat until the oil sizzles. Deep fry the rolls on each side until golden brown. Drain well on paper towels. Serve spring rolls with tamari sauce.

This recipe is another Russian *zakuski* staple. Try it with dark rye bread for an unusual sandwich filling. It also makes a delicious quiche when blended with sour cream, eggs and lots of fresh snipped chives.

Eggplant Caviar
makes 1 quarts

1 large	eggplant
1/4 c.	olive oil
1 c.	yellow onions, finely chopped
1 c.	green bell pepper, finely chopped
4	cloves garlic, peeled and crushed
1 1/2 c.	tomatoes, finely chopped
1 1/2 tsp.	honey
2 tsp.	salt
1/4 tsp.	cracked black pepper
2 Tbsp.	lemon juice

Roast the eggplant on a cookie sheet at 375 degrees for 45 minutes. Cool the eggplant, then peel and chop it finely . Saute the onion, pepper, and garlic in olive oil until softened. Add the chopped eggplant, tomato, honey, salt, and pepper. Simmer for 1 hour in a covered sauce pan. Remove the cover and continue simmering until the liquid evaporates, about 15 minutes. Stir occasionally. The final simmering takes about 30 minutes. Stir in the lemon juice and refrigerate until serving.

Dolmas
10 servings

1 c.	brown rice, cooked
1/4 c.	currants
1 c.	yellow onions, finely chopped
2 Tbsp.	extra virgin olive oil
1/2 c.	pinenuts, toasted
3 Tbsp.	parsley, finely chopped
3	cloves garlic, crushed
1/8 tsp.	cinnamon pinch allspice
1/2 tsp.	salt
1/4 tsp.	black pepper
1 jar	grape leaves (or 20 fresh, blanched for five minutes in boiling water)
2 Tbsp.	extra virgin olive oil, additional
1/2 c.	lemon juice
4 c.	water

Saute the onions in the two tablespoons of olive oil. Stir in the rice, currants, pinenuts, parsley, garlic and spices. Place a tablespoon of this filling in a horizontal line in the center of each flattened grape leaf. Roll each package starting from the bottom, folding the side edges toward the center as you roll. Each dolma should look like a tightly rolled stubby cigar approximately two inches long and 1 inch in diameter.

Place the dolmas in a baking pan and cover them with the additional olive oil, lemon juice and water. Place another pan or heavy oven-safe plate directly on top of the dolmas and place in a 375 degree oven for forty-five minutes. They also may be simmered on the stove in the pan if it is heavy-bottomed or made of stainless steel. Drain the dolmas and chill before serving.

Appetizers

Pecan Baked Chicken Drumettes
8 servings

2 dozen	chicken drumettes (chicken wings with wing tips removed)
2 c.	cracker or cornflake crumbs
1 c.	Parmesan cheese
1 c.	pecans, toasted and finely ground
5	eggs, beaten
2 c.	buttermilk

Combine the crumbs, Parmesan and ground pecans. Beat the eggs and buttermilk together. Roll the chicken drumettes in the crumb mixture, then dip each in the egg mixture allowing to drain slightly before rolling in the crumbs again. Place on a foil-lined baking sheet and sprinkle with salt and pepper. Bake at 400 degrees for one hour.

This is my friend and cooking compatriot, Jim Seitz's recipe for delicious chewy tofu. It is unbelievably easy!

Teriyaki Tofu
serves 8

2 lbs.	firm tofu
1 c.	tamari or soy sauce
1/2 c.	brown sugar
1 c.	water
1 Tbsp.	crushed red chilies
1 inch	fresh ginger, peeled and grated
2 Tbsp.	whole star anise
1/4 c.	peanut oil
4	cloves garlic, crushed

Whisk all ingredients except the tofu together and simmer for fifteen minutes. Cut firm tofu into 1 inch square cubes and marinate overnight in the marinade. Drain well and reserve the marinade in the refrigerator for the next batch. Place tofu cubes on a baking sheet and bake at 325 degrees for approximately one hour. Cool and keep refrigerated for happy snacking.

Smoked Tuna Mousse
serves 8

2 c.	smoked tuna
1 c.	cream cheese or yogurt cheese (see recipe next page)
1/2 c.	sour cream or plain yogurt
2 Tbsp.	snipped chives
2 Tbsp.	dill, chopped
4 dashes	Tabasco sauce
1/4 tsp.	white pepper

Finely chop smoked fish in a food processor or by hand with a sharp knife. Add cream cheese to food processor and blend until smooth. (If blending manually, whip cream cheese well and then blend in chopped fish.) Beat remaining ingredients together with the fish mixture in a bowl. Chill well and serve with cocktail bread, crostini, and breadsticks or pipe into hollowed out cucumber rounds, cherry tomatoes or romaine lettuce ribs.

Note: This recipe is equally delicious when other hot smoked seafood is used. Try smoked salmon, whitefish, sable, oysters or prawns.

Yogurt Cheese
makes 1 pint

1 qt. plain lowfat yogurt
cheesecloth
colander
string
large bowl

Place three layers of 12 by 12 inch square cheesecloth in the bottom of a colander. Pour the yogurt on the cheesecloth and allow the whey to drip into a bowl for 30 minutes. Gather up the ends of the cheesecloth and tie securely with the string. Place the colander in a bowl in the refrigerator overnight, pouring off the whey when it accumulates in the bowl. Allow the yogurt cheese to drain several days for a firmer texture.

Appetizers

Boursin
serves 4

1 c.	cream cheese
1/4 c.	mayonnaise
2 tsp.	dijon mustard
2 Tbsp.	chives, sliced
2 Tbsp.	dill, chopped
1 clove	garlic, minced
1 Tbsp.	tarragon, chopped
1 Tbsp.	parsley, chopped

Soften the cream cheese and blend in the mayonnaise, mustard and herbs. Chill. Serve as a spread with crackers and crisp apples or pears.

Boursin Dip
serves 4

1/4 c.	boursin cheese (see recipe previous page)
1/2 c.	sour cream
1/4 c.	mayonnaise

Blend ingredients together well and chill.

Note: For a lower calorie dip, use reduced fat mayonnaise and plain lowfat yogurt instead of the sour cream.

Dijon dip is a natural with raw vegetables, poached prawns or grilled tempeh. Serve in a hollowed out red cabbage bowl for a dramatic presentation.

Dijon Dip
serves 4

1/4 c.	Dijon mustard
1/2 c.	sour cream
3 Tbsp.	mayonnaise
1 Tbsp.	chives, thinly sliced

Blend all ingredients together well and chill.

joe saxe

Serve tapenade thinly spread on garlic-toasted baguette slices as an appetizer. It also is the base for many canapes garnished with roasted red pepper strips, green olives or a dab of whipped cream cheese.

Tapenade
serves 8

1 c.	calamata olives, pitted
4 whole	anchovy fillets
2 cloves	garlic, peeled and crushed
1/4 c.	capers
1/2 c.	cooked albacore tuna
2 Tbsp.	fresh oregano, finely chopped
1/8 tsp.	Tabasco sauce
1 tsp.	dry mustard
1/4 c.	lemon juice

Puree or mash all of the ingredients into a smooth paste. Refrigerate for up to 5 days.

The olive tree is surely the richest gift of heaven. I can scarcely expect bread. — Thomas Jefferson.

Appetizers

This recipe is a classic in falafel sandwiches. I fill an entire hollowed out red pepper with tahini sauce and surround it with raw vegetables for a fancy or informal party platter.

Tahini Sauce
serves 4

1 c.	tahini
1 c.	plain yogurt
1 clove	garlic, peeled and crushed
1/2 c.	lemon juice
1/4 c.	green onion, thinly sliced
1/4 c.	Italian parsley, chopped
1/2 tsp.	salt
1/4 tsp.	cayenne pepper
1/2 tsp.	cumin

Combine all of the ingredients well and refrigerate. Bring to room temperature before serving for the best flavor.

Roasted Garlic Spread
makes 1 pint

12	cloves garlic
2	russet potatoes
1/4 c.	olive oil
1 1/2 tsp.	salt
1/4 tsp.	white pepper
2 Tbsp.	basil, finely chopped

Place the unpeeled garlic cloves in a pie tin and roast in a 375 degree oven for 20 minuted or until lightly browned. Squeeze the softened garlic from their papery coverings and mash well with a fork. Peel, cube and boil the potatoes until very soft, about 25 minutes. Mash well with the garlic, olive oil, salt, pepper and basil. Serve this appetizer spread on toasted baguette slices, with crudites or dolloped on canapes with roasted red pepper and black olive slices.

In no department of life, in no place, should indifference be allowed to creep: into none less than the domain of cookery. — Yuan Mei

Appetizers

Roasted Red Pepper Spread
makes 1 pint

2	red bell peppers
1/2 c.	yellow onion, thinly sliced
1 Tbsp.	olive oil
1 tsp.	salt
1/4 tsp.	white pepper
2 Tbsp.	sour cream or lowfat plain yogurt

Roast the peppers whole either over an open gas flame or in a 400 degree oven. When roasting over a flame, turn frequently until all of the exposed skin is charred. Roasting in the oven takes approximately 40 minutes turning the peppers about halfway through. Place the roasted peppers in a plastic bag to allow the skin to "sweat" for easier peeling. Peel the peppers when cool and rinse with cold water. The skins usually slip right off with light rubbing, but may need extra roasting time for unusually thick or partially charred skins. Saute the onion in the olive oil until soft but not browned. Puree the peppers and onion in a food processor or blender until smooth. Stir in the salt, pepper and sour cream and chill. Serve as a dip for vegetables, crackers or as a spread for canapes.

Guacamole
serves 8

6	avocadoes
1/2 c.	lemon juice
1 c.	tomatoes, chopped
1/2 c.	onion, sliced
1/2 c.	cilantro, chopped
2	jalapenos, chopped
6	cloves garlic, minced
1 tsp.	salt
1/2 tsp.	white pepper

Mash the avocadoes with the lemon juice. Add the remaining ingredients and stir well. Chill.

Entrees

Oven-Fried Chicken	166
Ratatouille	167
Lasagne Verde	168
Bstilla	170
Stuffed Cabbage	172
Tamales with Chicken, Chilies and Muenster Cheese	174
Vegetarian Tamales	176
Chicken Adobo	178
White Bean Chili	179
Vegetarian Risotto	180
Pecan Crisp Chicken	181
Twice Baked Sweet Potatoes	182
Russian Vegetable Pie	183
Tsimmes	184
Nan's Lukshen Kugel	185
Tachin	186
Melitzanopita (Eggplant Pie)	188
Baked Stuffed Eggplant	189
Salmon Croquettes	190
Tortilla Stack	191
Mexican Chicken Pie	192
Szechuan Noodles	193
Barley Pilaf	194

Entrees

For this section, I have selected easy-to-prepare dishes from our repertoire of dinner specialties. The ingredients for these entrees can be purchased in most grocery stores (with the exception, perhaps, of corn husks for the tamales, basmati rice, dried cranberries, or phyllo dough). Specialty or ethnic markets carry a myriad of unusual and exciting items with which the adventurous cook can experiment. Sometimes I dream up new recipes while browsing in the ethnic neighborhood markets in San Francisco and end up buying more stuff than I actually need for the recipe at hand. A pantry full of exotic ingredients will allow great imaginative freedom for the plan-ahead cook.

I recommend preparing a greater quantity of sauces or cooked dishes when you find yourself in "cooking mode." Dispatch the extras to the freezer or fridge for a practically effortless foray into the realm of dinnertime frenzy on a busy night. For example, when making Mexican chicken pie for a Sunday night get-together, make extra mushroom sauce to be used in chicken tetrazzini later in the week or in sherried cream of mushroom soup for lunch the next day. Cook extra chicken and freeze the chopped or shredded meat for use in a quick stir-fry (with orange-tamari sauce), in chicken salad, creamy chicken garbanzo soup, or "fist food" filling. The possibilities are limitless when you get accustomed to planning ahead for future meals.

As with all the recipes in this book, quality — the freshness and purity of the ingredients — is important. I use only free-range poultry and eggs at the restaurant for several reasons, the most essential of which is their extraordinary flavor. Natural ranching methods also result in a healthier product—no artificial feed, drugs, or hormones are used to pollute the food which the consumer ingests. Organic farming follows the same sound practice of eliminating that which is unnatural from the food-growing process. No chemical fertilizers, sprays or waxes, thank you! The lower yield of most organic farms (caused by the loss of some of the crop to insects) will invariably result in a slightly higher price. In my opinion, the higher price is worth the peace of mind to be able to eat food that is poison-free.

Oven-Fried Chicken
Serves 4

1	whole fryer, quartered
4 c.	cornflake crumbs
1 Tbsp.	paprika
1/2 tsp.	white pepper
1 tsp.	salt
1 c.	safflower oil

Wash the quartered chicken very well and pat dry. Set aside. Combine the crumbs, paprika, pepper and salt. Brush the chicken pieces with safflower oil and dip in the crumb mixture. Place in a foil-lined pan and bake at 375 degrees for 1 1/2 hours.

Some sensible person once remarked that you spend the whole of your life either in your bed or in your shoes. Having done the best you can by shoes and bed, devote all the time and resources at your disposal to the building up of a fine kitchen. It will be, as it should be, the most comforting and comfortable room in the house. — Elizabeth David, French Country Cooking 1951

Ratatouille
Serves 4

1	eggplant, peeled and cubed
1/2 c.	olive oil
1/4 c.	melted butter
6	cloves garlic, chopped
2 c.	yellow onion, chopped
2 c.	zucchini, sliced
2 c.	tomatoes, chopped
2 c.	peppers, chopped
1/2 c.	white wine
2 tsp.	salt
1/2 tsp.	white pepper
1/2 c.	basil, oregano, and parsley, chopped

Saute the eggplant cubes in the olive oil. Add the butter, garlic, and onions. Saute for 10 minutes more. Add the zucchini, tomatoes, peppers and wine. Simmer until soft, about 1/2 hour. Add salt, pepper and herbs.

Note: Ratatouille is a typical omelette filling. Pair it with feta cheese, or for the quintessential meal, an imported French chevre.

Lasagne Verde
Serves 8 hearty appetites

Filling:

2 lbs.	part-skim ricotta cheese
4	blocks tofu
3	eggs, beaten
1 c.	Parmesan cheese
1 c.	mozzarella, shredded

Mash together all of the ingredients.

15	spinach lasagne noodles, cooked until soft in boiling water.
2 c.	pesto sauce (see recipe page 213)
2 c.	mushrooms, sliced and sauteed in olive oil
4 c.	spinach, washed, chopped and sauteed in olive oil
1 c.	provolone or mozzarella cheese, shredded

Spread about 1/2 c. pesto sauce on the bottom of a baking pan. Layer 5 lasagna noodles across the bottom. Spread 3 c. of the filling on top of the noodles. Add the mushrooms evenly on top of the filling and top with 5 more lasagne noodles. Carefully spread 1/2 c. pesto on top of these noodles and add the remaining filling evenly. Place the well-drained spinach on the filling and top with the remaining noodles. Spread the pesto sauce over the top of the lasagne and sprinkle with the shredded cheese. Bake at 350 degrees for 35 - 40 minutes, or until the cheese is lightly browned and bubbly.

(continued)

Country Fare
Vegetarian
Or not! Heavenly haven
Organically grown — Bitt 4/23/92

Entrees

Note: Lasagne filling may be used in a variety of entrees. Stuff manicotti (large pasta tubes) with filling, then bake with marinara sauce and grated cheese. We often get requests for our cannelloni at the restaurant. Fill uncooked won ton wrappers (available in the produce section of most grocery stores) with 2 Tbsp. each of lasagne filling. Roll each wrapper loosely around the filling into a long cylinder. Place rows of cannelloni in a baking pan on a layer of marinara sauce. Cover with more sauce and bake at 350 degrees for 30 minutes. Serve three cannelloni per person with a stripe of pesto, marinara and bechamel sauce on each cannelloni.

A classic Moroccan bstilla is a pigeon pie wrapped in phyllo dough and served sprinkled with powdered sugar. We forgo the pigeon and the sugar at Country Fare, but the flavor is equally exotic.

Bstilla
Serves 8

1 c.	celery, chopped
1 c.	onions, chopped
4 Tbsp.	clarified butter
4 c.	cooked chicken, chopped
2	eggs, beaten
1 c.	buttermilk
1/2 tsp.	salt
1/4 tsp.	white pepper
1/4 tsp.	cinnamon
2 tsp.	saffron, dissolved in 1 Tbsp. hot water to release flavor & color
1/2 c.	cilantro, chopped
1 1/2 c.	almonds, blanched, toasted and chopped
1 pkg.	frozen phyllo dough, thawed
1/2 c.	butter, clarified or melted

Saute the celery and onions in the clarified butter. Stir in the cooked chicken, eggs, buttermilk, salt, pepper, cinnamon, saffron solution and cilantro. Simmer, stirring often until the liquid is absorbed.

(continued)

To prepare individual bstillas, layer two sheets of phyllo dough, buttering each well. Cut the sheets into six equal parts and press one section, buttered side down, into a one cup ramekin. Place 1/4 cup of the chicken mixture in the ramekin and layer with another section of buttered phyllo dough. Sprinkle this layer with 2 Tbsp. of chopped almonds and top with another section of phyllo, pressing evenly to pack the mold. Repeat the layers of chicken, phyllo dough, almonds and phyllo twice more ending with a layer of phyllo dough. Press the entire mold well and unmold onto a baking tray. Brush the top well with melted butter and prepare the remaining bstillas. Bake at 400 degrees for 15 - 20 minutes or until browned and crispy.

Stuffed Cabbage

Makes 12 cabbage rolls-serves 6

1	large head of green cabbage
1 c.	yellow onion, chopped
3	cloves garlic, crushed
1/4 c.	carrot, grated
1/4 c.	celery, chopped
1/4 c.	safflower oil
1/4 c.	sunflower seeds, toasted
1/2 lb.	tofu, mashed
2 c.	brown rice, cooked
1/4 c.	raisins
2 Tbsp.	tamari
1/2 c.	marinara sauce (see recipe page 206)
1/4 c.	cider vinegar

Remove the core of the green cabbage and parboil for 10 minutes or until the leaves are soft. Remove the outer leaves carefully and save for rolling around the filling. Saute the onions, garlic, carrots and celery in the safflower oil. Transfer to a big bowl and add the sunflower seeds, cashews, tofu, brown rice, raisins, tamari, marinara sauce and cider vinegar. Place 1/4 c. of the filling on stem end of the cabbage leaf (trim the core if too bulky) and roll like a burrito. Place seam side down in a baking dish 6 to a layer and make 2 layers. Pour some sauce (recipe below) on the rolls, and bake for 30 minutes at 350 degrees.

(continued)

Sauce

1 c.	marinara sauce (see recipe page 206)
1/4 c.	cider vinegar
2 Tbsp.	molasses
1 Tbsp.	tamari
1 Tbsp.	honey
1/2 tsp.	white pepper
1 c.	water

Blend the marinara sauce with the cider vinegar. Heat the sauce until bubbly. Add the molasses, tamari, honey, white pepper and water.

Tamales with Chicken, Chilies and Muenster Cheese

makes 1 dozen 6" long tamales

Tamale Dough:

1 lb.	grits or polenta, finely ground in food processor
2 tsp.	salt
1 c.	butter or chicken fat
1 1/2 c.	chicken broth
1/2 tsp.	baking powder
1 pkg.	corn husks

Filling:

4 c.	cooked chicken, shredded
2 tsp.	garlic, minced
1/2 c.	onion, minced
6	roasted Anaheim chilies, finely chopped
1 1/2 c.	Muenster cheese, shredded

Stir the polenta and broth into the melted butter or fat. Beat for three minutes until well blended. Mix in the baking powder. In a separate bowl, stir together the chicken, onion, garlic, chilies and cheese.

Assembly

Soak the corn husks in hot water for twenty minutes to make them pliable. Snip the ends off the corn husks and fill the inner cavity with 4 Tbsp. of the tamale dough. Spread the dough to a 1/2" thickness and fill with 3 Tbsp. filling. Spread 3 Tbsp. of the dough on top of the filling and top with another corn husk. Fold the bottom corn husk lengthwise to form a closed cylinder and fold the ends up to close. Wrap and tie the tamale closed with a strip of corn husk. Heat water in the bottom of a steamer to a rolling boil and line the top of the steamer with corn husks. Place wrapped tamales standing up in the steamer and cover with more husks. Steam for 2 hours until the dough feels firm. Keep a pot of simmering water handy to replenish the boiling water in the steamer bottom.

Vegetarian Tamales
makes 1 dozen

2 c.	water
1 Tbsp.	olive oil
6 c.	masa harina or cornmeal, finely ground
1 tsp.	salt
1	package corn husks, softened for 30 minutes in warm water and drained
1 c.	broccoli, chopped
1 c.	cauliflower, chopped
2 c.	carrots, peeled and chopped
1 c.	yellow onions, chopped
1 c.	zucchini, chopped
12	cloves garlic, peeled and chopped
2	jalapeno peppers, finely chopped
1/4 c.	olive oil
2 c.	firm tofu, crumbled
3 c.	soy or regular Monterey jack cheese, grated
2 c.	green olives
2 tsp.	ground cumin
1/2 tsp.	white pepper
2 tsp.	salt
1/4 tsp.	cayenne pepper

(continued)

Blend the first 4 ingredients together. Spread 1/4 c. of this dough on the wide part of 24 husks. Saute the vegetables in the olive oil until tender. Blend all of the remaining ingredients with the vegetables. Place 1/4 c. of this mixture on 12 of the cornmeal covered husks. Top with the other husks wide end to narrow end. Fold the narrow ends over and tie with thin strips of the leftover husks to form a package. Place corn husks to cover the bottom of a heavy steamer or other wide bottomed pan. Add 3 cups of water and gently place the tamales in the pot. Cover with additional husks and cover the pot. Bring to a boil and lower the heat to medium to create lots of steam. Let the tamales cook for one hour, adding hot water if necessary to prevent scorching. When ready, tamales spring back when poked. Snip the ties and unwrap the tamales to serve. Serve hot with salsa fresca (see recipe page 203) and sour cream.

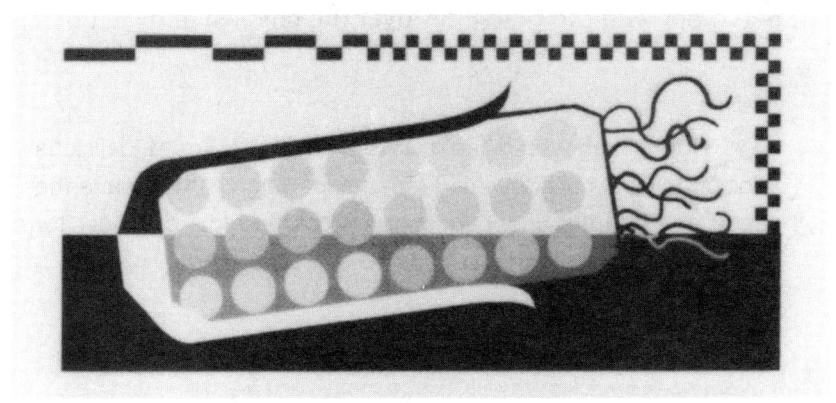

Chicken Adobo
Serves 8

2	whole chickens, quartered
3/4 c.	tamari or soy sauce
3/4 c.	white wine vinegar
3 c.	chicken or turkey stock
1	bay leaf
2 tsp.	peppercorns
6	cloves garlic

Place the chicken pieces in a large soup pot. Cover with the tamari, vinegar, and stock. Put the bay leaf, peppercorns and garlic in a cheese-cloth bag and add to the pot. Add water to bring the level of liquid over the chicken if necessary. Simmer over a medium heat for 1 1/2 hours, or until tender. Remove the chicken from the pot and keep warm. Take out cheesecloth bag. Skim the fat from the top of the gravy. Stir in 1/2 c. arrowroot blended with 1/4 c. cold water to thicken the sauce. Serve hot with the rich gravy over the chicken and steamed rice.

Note: Leftover diced chicken adobo makes a delicious addition to Thai chicken salad (see recipe page 111) or save the sauce and add the chopped meat, stock and lots of ginger for an exquisite soup.

I want you all to know that I don't bring just anyone to this place! Special places for special people! — Norm L. 5/5/92

This chili is delicious served with a garnish of chopped olives and grated cheese. Pair a big steaming bowl of chili with cornbread for a satisfying supper.

White Bean Chili
serves 8

6 c.	white beans, soaked overnight
2	bay leaves
1/4 c.	olive oil
6	cloves garlic, peeled and chopped
2	jalapeno peppers, chopped
1 c.	yellow onions, chopped
2 c.	red bell pepper, chopped
4 c.	tomatoes, chopped
2 tsp.	salt
1/4 tsp.	white pepper
1/4 tsp.	cayenne pepper
1 Tbsp.	paprika
1/2 c.	white wine

Cook the beans with the bay leaves in fresh water to cover until soft. Drain well. Saute the garlic, jalapenos, onion, peppers, and tomatoes in the olive oil for five minutes. Add the beans and stir in the salt, pepper, cayenne, paprika, and wine. Simmer all together stirring often for one hour.

Beans are highly nutritious and satisfying, they can also be delicious if and when properly prepared, and they possess over all vegetables the great advantage of being just as good, if not better, when kept waiting, an advantage in the case of people whose disposition or occupation makes it difficult for them to be punctual at mealtime. — Andre Simon, The Concise Encyclopedia of Gastronomy 1952

Vegetarian Risotto
serves 6

4 c.	broccoli, chopped
6 c.	mushrooms, sliced
1 c.	yellow onions, chopped
6	cloves garlic, peeled and chopped
1/4 c.	olive oil
5 c.	water
2 c.	risotto (Italian arborio rice)
6	eggs, beaten
1/2 c.	Parmesan cheese
2 tsp.	salt
1/2 tsp.	white pepper
3 c.	tomatoes, chopped
1/4 c.	basil, chopped
4 c.	provolone cheese, grated
1 c.	pine nuts, toasted

Saute the vegetables in the olive oil until crisp tender. Add the water and bring to a boil. Stir in the risotto and simmer for 30 minutes, stirring occasionally until the water is absorbed. Blend the eggs, Parmesan cheese, herbs, tomatoes, salt, and pepper and stir into the hot risotto. Put in an olive-oiled baking pan and sprinkle with the provolone cheese and pinenuts. Bake at 350 degrees for 40 minutes or until brown.

Entrees

Pecan Crisp Chicken
serves 4

1	whole fryer, cut into quarters
1 c.	cracker crumbs
1/2 c.	Parmesan cheese
1/2 c.	pecans, toasted and finely ground
3	eggs, beaten
2 c.	buttermilk

Combine the cracker crumbs, Parmesan cheese and pecans. Beat the eggs and buttermilk together. Roll the chicken pieces in the crumb mixture, dip in the egg mixture and then dip in the crumbs again. Place in a hotel pan and bake at 400 degrees for 1 hour.

Twice Baked Sweet Potatoes
serves 6

6	large sweet potatoes, washed well and pierced all over with a fork
3 c.	turkey breast, cooked and chopped
2 c.	provolone cheese, grated
1 c.	dried cranberries, soaked in hot water for 30 minutes (or 1/2 c. whole berry cranberry sauce, well-drained)
2 c.	pecans, toasted and chopped
1/4 c.	sherry
2 tsp.	salt
1/2 tsp.	white pepper

Bake the sweet potatoes at 400 degrees for 45-55 minutes. Scoop out the pulp and mash. Mix the sweet potato pulp with the turkey, cheese, cranberries, pecans, sherry, salt, and pepper. Stuff the filling back into the potato skins and bake at 350 degrees for 40 minutes. This dish is very tasty served with a drizzle of mornay sauce (see recipe page 210).

Dining is and always was a great artistic opportunity.
— Frank Lloyd Wright

Russian Vegetable Pie
serves 6

2 Tbsp.	unsalted butter
2 c.	green cabbage, shredded
1 c.	leeks, sliced and washed well
2 c.	mushrooms, sliced
1 c.	carrots, sliced
5	eggs, beaten
1/2 c.	sour cream
1/4 c.	half&half
1/4 c.	unbleached flour
1 tsp.	salt
1/4 tsp.	white pepper
1/4 c.	dill, chopped
	pie pastry (see recipe page 243)

Saute the vegetables in butter. Blend the remaining ingredients together and pour into a purchased or homemade pie shell. Bake at 375 degrees for 35-40 minutes or until browned and set. Allow to cool for five minutes before slicing.

Promises and pie-crust are made to be broken. — Jonathan Swift, Polite Conversation 1738

Tsimmes
serves 8

8 c.	sweet potatoes, peeled and cut in chunks
4 c.	carrots, sliced
2	tart apples, peeled and sliced
1/2 c.	yellow onions, chopped
1/2 c.	dates, pitted and chopped
1/2 c.	gold raisins
3 Tbsp.	lemon juice
1 tsp.	salt
1/2 tsp.	cinnamon
1/2 c.	orange juice
1/2 c.	honey

Mix all of the ingredients together and place in a buttered baking pan. Sprinkle with 1 cup crumb topping (see recipe page 19). Cover with foil and bake at 350 degrees for 2 hours. Uncover and bake 1/2 hour or until the top is browned.

Nan's Lukshen Kugel
serves 4

2 c.	cornflake crumbs
4	eggs, beaten
1 c.	sugar or fructose
1 tsp.	cinnamon
1/2 c.	sour cream
2 c.	cottage cheese
1/2 c.	milk
4 Tbsp.	unsalted butter, melted
8 c.	ribbon noodles, cooked and drained
2 Tbsp.	cold unsalted butter

Butter a baking pan and sprinkle with 1 cup of the cornflake crumbs. In a food processor, beat together the eggs, fructose, cinnamon, sour cream, cottage cheese, milk, and butter. Mix with the cooked noodles and place in the baking pan. Sprinkle the top with the remaining cornflake crumbs and dot with butter. Bake uncovered at 400 degrees for 1 hour or until browned.

Note: Leftover kugel is outstanding when thinly sliced and fried quickly in butter to serve as a breakfast side dish.

Love is grand, but love with lukshen (noodles) is even better. — Yiddish proverb

Tachin

serves 8

1 c.	yellow onions, chopped
4 c.	basmati rice
6 c.	water
1/2 tsp.	saffron
2	chickens, cooked & cubed
2 c.	plain lowfat yogurt
1 1/2 tsp.	salt
1/4 tsp.	white pepper
1 c.	chicken stock
1/2 tsp.	saffron

Place the chopped onions, rice, water and 1/4 tsp. saffron in an ovenproof casserole and let stand for ten minutes to allow saffron to dissolve. Stir well, cover the pan tightly and place in a 400 degree oven for 1 1/2 hours. Meanwhile, bake or poach the chickens, cool and cube the meat. (If poaching the chickens, cook for one hour, remove the chickens and continue cooking the broth to reduce it by half. Strain this stock and use in the tachin recipe. If baking the chickens, which provides a richer flavor, bake along with the rice in a separate pan for approximately 1 1/2 hours. Debone the chickens, cube the meat and cover the bones with water to simmer for stock.)

(continued)

One cannot think well, love well, sleep well, if one has not dined well. — Virginia Woolf

Allow the remaining saffron to dissolve in 1 cup of the chicken stock for ten minutes. Stir well and add the yogurt, salt and pepper. To assemble the tachin, butter two loaf pans well and place half of the cooked rice evenly in the bottom of each. Cover with half of the chopped chicken meat and then with half of the yogurt sauce. Top each loaf with the remaining rice and finish with the yogurt sauce. Poke several holes through both loaves to allow the top layer of yogurt sauce to permeate the loaves. Bake uncovered in a 375 degree oven for 45 minutes or until the loaves start to pull away from the sides of the pans.

Melitzanopita (Eggplant Pie)
serves 6

4	large eggplants, peeled and sliced
1 c.	flour, unbleached
1 tsp.	salt
1/4 tsp.	pepper
1/4 c.	olive oil
1 c.	yellow onions, chopped
6	cloves garlic, minced
4 c.	tomatoes, chopped
1 tsp.	salt
1/4 tsp.	white pepper
1/4 c.	basil, chopped
1/4 c.	oregano, chopped
1/2 tsp.	cinnamon
2 c.	plain yogurt
2 c.	ricotta cheese
1 Tbsp.	sesame seeds
2 c.	feta cheese, crumbled
1/4 c.	Italian parsley, chopped

Dredge the eggplant slices in the flour mixed with salt and pepper. Use the olive oil for grilling the eggplant slices on both sides until golden brown. Set aside. Saute the onion, garlic, and tomatoes in additional olive oil. Stir in the herbs and cinnamon. Keep warm. Blend the yogurt, ricotta, and sesame seeds together. In a baking pan layer 1/3 of the eggplant slices, 1/3 of the tomato sauce, and 1/3 of the cheese mixture. Repeat 2 more times ending with the cheese mixture. Sprinkle 2 cups of the crumbled feta on top. Bake 40 minutes at 350 degrees. Garnish with chopped parsley.

Pure men like pure food which gives true health, balanced mentality, sustaining strength, life long enough to search. Pure food which has delicate taste, soothes, nourishes and brings them joy. Pure food that promotes the knowledge of God. — Bhagavad Gita

Baked Stuffed Eggplant
serves 4

1/4 c.	olive oil
1/4 c.	green pepper, chopped
1/4 c.	red pepper, chopped
2 c.	celery, finely chopped
4	cloves garlic, minced
2 c.	bread, cubed
1/4 c.	Italian parsley, chopped
1/4 c.	oregano, chopped
1/4 c.	basil, chopped
1/4 c.	Parmesan cheese
2 c.	jack cheese, grated
1 tsp.	salt
1/4 tsp.	white pepper
2 large	eggplants

Halve the eggplants and bake cut side down for 35 minutes at 350 degrees. Scoop out the pulp and chop finely. Save the eggplant skin "shells". Saute the first 4 ingredients in the olive oil until tender. Blend all of the remaining ingredients together and stuff into the eggplant skins. Bake at 350 degrees for 40 minutes or until golden brown.

Salmon Croquettes
serves 4

1 lbs.	salmon, poached and flaked (or 1 one lb. can of salmon, cleaned of skin and bones)
1/2 c.	green onions, sliced with 2 inches of the green tops
2 Tbsp.	fresh dill, chopped (or 1 Tbsp. dried dill weed)
2	russett potatoes, peeled, boiled, and mashed
1 tsp.	salt
1/4 tsp.	white pepper
1	egg, beaten
1 c.	soft bread crumbs

Mash the cooked salmon, onions, potatoes, dill, and salt and pepper together. Shape into 3 ounce patties. Dip each patty into beaten egg and roll in the bread crumbs. Fry in a scant amount of canola oil or clarified butter on both sides until golden brown, approximately three minutes per side. Serve with tartar sauce (see recipe page 215).

Note: Serve salmon croquettes for breakfast with roasted or grilled potatoes.

The most important activity in human life is eating. As any community progresses, its diet is the most salient guide to its refinement. — A.H.Sharar

Tortilla Stack

serves 6

1 1/2 lb.	ground turkey
1/4 c.	olive oil
1/2 c.	roasted chilies, diced
1	jalapeno, diced
1 c.	yellow onion, diced
4	cloves garlic, minced
4 c.	tomato puree
1 Tbsp.	cumin
1 Tbsp.	coriander
2 Tbsp.	chili powder
2 tsp.	salt
1/2 tsp.	black pepper
4 c.	pinto beans, cooked
18	corn tortillas
1 1/2 c.	Monterey jack cheese

Saute the ground turkey in the olive oil. Add the chilies, onion and garlic and saute for 5 minutes more. Add the tomato puree, spices and beans and simmer for 30 minutes. Stir in the salt and pepper. Fry three tortillas per order until crisp. Layer a tortilla, sauce, tortilla, sauce, tortilla, sauce and finish with grated cheese. Heat in the oven or microwave to melt the cheese. Garnish with chopped olives, sour cream and avocado slices.

Mexican Chicken Pie

serves 4

1	whole fryer, cut into quarters
12	corn tortillas
1 c.	mushroom sauce (see recipe page 211)
2 Tbsp.	olive oil
2	Anaheim chilies, roasted, peeled and pureed
1 c.	yellow onion, pureed
1	jalapeno, finely chopped
4	cloves garlic, pureed
1 tsp.	salt
1/2 tsp.	white pepper
2 c.	Monterey jack cheese, grated

Saute the pureed chilies, onion, garlic and jalapenos in the olive oil. Stir in the salt and pepper. Bake the chicken for 1 hour. Cool, then debone and shred the meat. Tear the tortillas into 2 inch strips and place 1/3 of the tortilla strips in the bottom of an olive-oiled baking pan. Place 1/2 of the shredded chicken meat on the tortilla strips and pour on 1/3 of the mushroom and 1/3 of the chili sauces. Layer with 1/3 more tortillas, the remaining chicken and 1/3 more of each sauce. Finish with the last 1/3 of the tortilla strips and the remaining sauces. Sprinkle with the cheese and bake at 375 degrees for 1 hour.

I'm full, fed and happy after a long day's work. Thanks for doing the dishes. — Catherine

Szechuan Noodles
serves 4

1 lb.	spaghetti, udon or ramen noodles, cooked, drained and tossed with:
1 Tbsp.	peanut oil
2 Tbsp.	peanut oil
1/4 c.	green onions, sliced
1/2 c.	celery, sliced
1/2 c.	bok choy, sliced
1/4 c.	peanuts, toasted and chopped
1/4 c.	sesame seeds, toasted
1/4 c.	tamari
2 Tbsp.	cider vinegar
2 tsp.	honey
1/4 tsp.	Tabasco
2 Tbsp.	catsup

Stir-fry the green onions, celery and bok choy in the peanut oil for 1 minute. Add the remaining ingredients and simmer for 3 minutes. Add the noodles and toss to coat with the sauce and heat through.

Barley Pilaf
serves 4

1/2 c.	yellow onions, chopped
2 Tbsp.	butter
2 c.	barley
3 c.	water or stock
1 tsp.	salt
1/4 tsp.	white pepper
1/4 c.	parsley, chopped
1/4 c.	sesame seeds, toasted

Saute the onions in the butter. Add to the barley, water, salt and pepper in a deep baking pan. Cover and bake at 400 degrees for 1 1/2 to 2 hours. When all of the liquid is absorbed, stir in the herbs and sesame seeds.

Sauces & Condiments

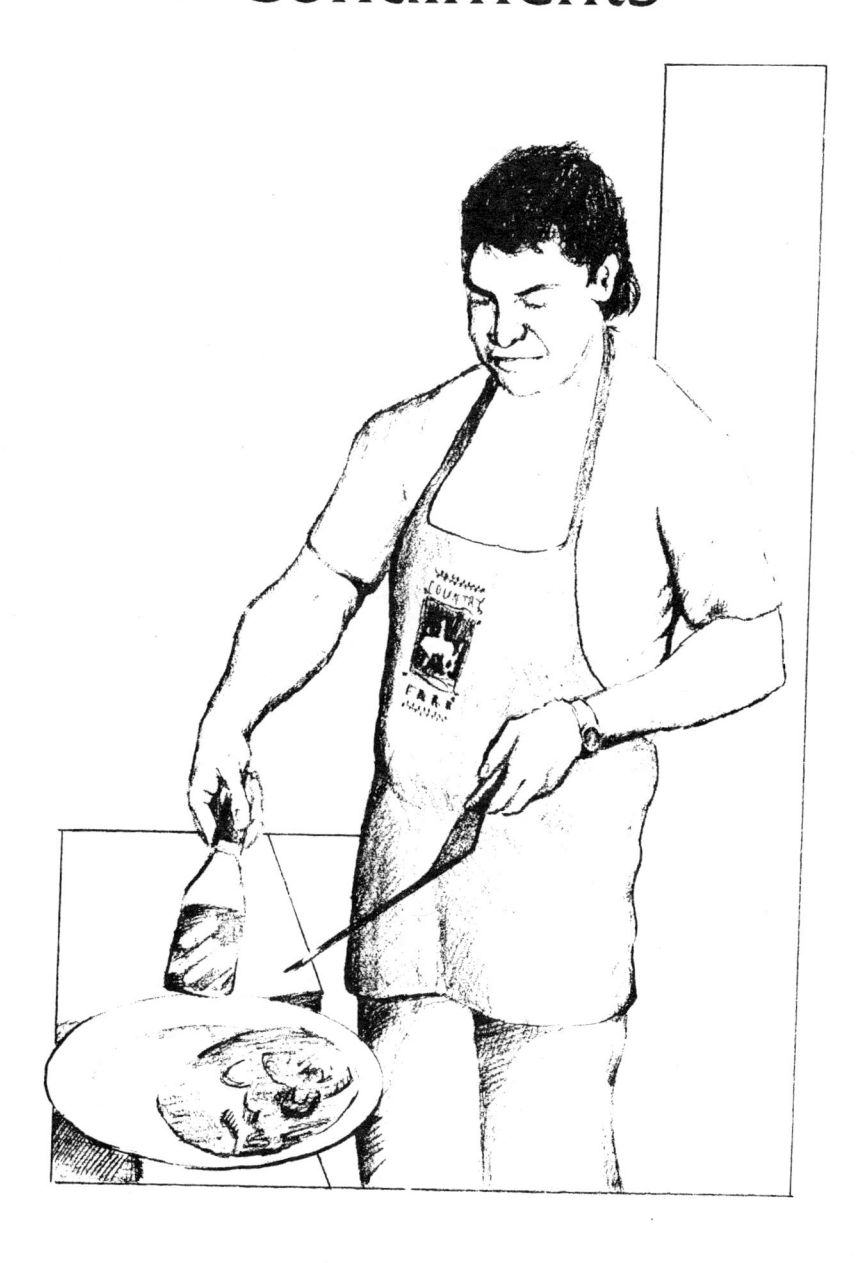

Curry Paste 198
Cucumber Raita 199
Sweet Potato Raita 200
Mango Chutney 201
Cranberry Chutney 202
Salsa Fresca 203
Corn Salsa 204
Orange Tamari Sauce 205
Marinara Sauce 206
Barbecue Sauce 207
Spicy Peanut Sauce 208
Pomegranate-Walnut Sauce 209
Mornay Sauce 210
Mushroom Sauce 211
Cilantro Sour Cream 212
Pesto Sauce 213
Roasted Red Pepper Sauce 214
Tartar Sauce 215
Cranberry Ketchup 216
Nectarine Mustard 217
Apple Sauce 218
Honey Yogurt Sauce 219
Red Onion Marmalade 220
Raspberry-Rhubarb Conserves 221

Sauces & Condiments

As you will notice, many of the recipes contained in this section are repeated in a few recipes throughout this book. The beauty of sauces is that they can be frozen and stored easily for future uses. Most can be prepared with a minimum of time and effort. Please keep in mind that only the freshest and best ingredients should be used in making a sauce: the freshest organic basil in pesto sauce, the tastiest organic tomatoes in marinara sauce, the freshest milk in white sauce. The quality of the ingredients will determine the success of any recipe.

Use curry paste to scramble tofu or tempeh for a deliciously unusual breakfast. A jar of this paste in your refrigerator will be handy for last minute dinner ideas. Stir it into sauteed vegetables and chicken, seafood, or tofu and serve with steamed cooked rice and any of the chutneys and raitas in the sauce section. Curry paste adds a wonderful depth to soups and a spicy note to salad dressings or composed salads.

Curry Paste
makes 1 1/2 pints

2 c.	yellow onions, sliced
12	cloves garlic, peeled and sliced
2	jalapeno peppers, chopped
1/2 inch	fresh ginger, peeled and grated
1 Tbsp.	cumin
1 Tbsp.	ground coriander
2 Tbsp.	mild curry powder
2 tsp.	salt
1 tsp.	white pepper
1/4 tsp.	cayenne powder

Puree the onion, garlic, jalapenos, and ginger in a food processor. Stir in all of the remaining ingredients and refrigerate until ready to use. Keeps refrigerated up to 2 weeks.

Cucumber Raita
makes 1 quart

1	cucumber, peeled, deseeded and chopped finely
3 c.	plain yogurt
1 tsp.	cumin
1 tsp.	salt
1 c.	fresh cilantro, finely chopped

Blend all of the ingredients together to create a thick sauce. Refrigerate for up to 1 week.

Sweet Potato Raita
Makes 1 quart

2 c.	sweet potatoes, peeled, cooked and mashed
2 c.	plain yogurt
1/2 c.	shredded coconut
1/4 tsp.	jalapeno, finely chopped
1 tsp.	yellow mustard seeds
1/2 Tbsp.	salt
1/2 Tbsp.	lemon juice
1/4 c.	cilantro, chopped
1/4 tsp.	powdered ginger

Mash all ingredients together well. Chill for a refreshing condiment to pair with spicy curries.

This chutney is a frequently requested recipe at Country Fare. It is incredibly easy to prepare and has a myriad of practical uses. We serve it with curries, spicy dahl soup (see recipe page 70), grilled meats, sandwiches, hors d'ouevres, etc., etc., etc. Experiment and enjoy!

Mango Chutney
makes 2 quarts

3 large	fresh mangoes, peeled and chopped
1/4 c.	yellow onions, finely chopped
3/4 c.	candied or crystallized ginger, finely chopped
2 c.	brown sugar
1/2 c.	rice wine vinegar
1 tsp.	salt
1/4 tsp.	ground cloves
1/4 tsp.	cinnamon
1/8 tsp.	cayenne pepper

Place all of the ingredients in a heavy-bottomed sauce pan. Simmer for 1 hour, stirring often to prevent sticking. The chutney can be canned in glass jars in a traditional hot water bath, or refrigerate the chutney for up to 6 months.

The kitchen is a country in which there are always discoveries to be made. — Grimod de la Reyniere, Almanach des Gourmands 1804

Chutney is a delightful condiment when used in untraditional ways. Blend your favorite chutney with cream cheese for a tangy spread on toast, bagels or muffins. We love this chutney with turkey on sandwiches or with cheddar cheese and chopped walnuts for simple and colorful canapes. Experiment with tastes, textures, and colors to create your own culinary masterpiece.

Cranberry Chutney
makes 1 1/2 quarts

2 c.	fructose or sugar
1 c.	cider vinegar
4 c.	fresh or frozen cranberries
1 tsp.	cinnamon
1/2 tsp.	nutmeg
1/2 tsp.	ground ginger powder
2 Tbsp.	candied or crystallized ginger, chopped
1/4 tsp.	ground cloves
1 Tbsp.	fresh ginger, grated

Heat the sugar and vinegar in a heavy-bottomed pot until bubbles appear along the periphery of the pan. Add the cranberries and cook vigorously until they begin to pop. Stir in the spices, candied and fresh gingers and turn the heat down to low. Simmer for 30 minutes. Can jars of cranberry chutney in a hot water bath following canning instructions or refrigerate for up to 6 months.

Sauces & Condiments

Salsa Fresca
makes 1 quart

3	ripe, but firm medium-sized tomatoes
1/2 c.	yellow onion, finely chopped
6	cloves garlic, crushed
1	small serrano chili or 1/2 jalapeno pepper
1/2 c.	red bell pepper, finely chopped
1 Tbsp.	extra virgin olive oil
2 Tbsp.	lemon juice
2 tsp.	salt
1/2 c.	cilantro, coarsely chopped

Hold the tomatoes with tongs over a gas flame or roast briefly on a grill until the skin begins to blister all over. Remove from the flame and peel while still warm. Remove the seeds and chop finely. Toss the chopped tomatoes with the remaining ingredients and let stand for one hour to let the flavors blend. Use immediately or chill until ready to use.

To eat is human, to digest divine.
—Mark Twain

Corn Salsa

Makes 1 quarts

4 c.	fresh or frozen corn kernels
2 c.	bell peppers, finely chopped
1	jalapeno, finely chopped
4	cloves garlic, minced
1/4 c.	red onion, finely minced
1/4 c.	lemon juice
1/4 c.	cilantro, chopped
3/4 tsp.	salt
1/4 tsp.	white pepper

Stir all ingredients together well and chill until serving time.

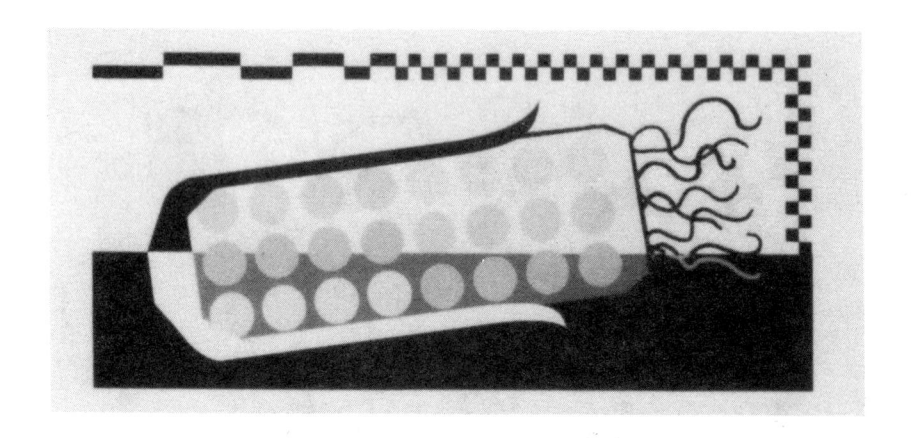

Sauces & Condiments

Orange Tamari Sauce
Makes 1 pint

1/2 c.	tamari
1/2 c.	sesame oil
1 c.	orange juice
1 Tbsp.	ginger, grated
1 Tbsp.	garlic, minced

Blend ingredients well. Shake well before using each time.

Sauces are to cookery what the gamut is to the composition of music, as it is by the arrangement of notes that harmony is produced, so should the ingredients in the sauce be nicely blended, and that delightful concord should exist, which would equally delight the palate, as a masterpiece of a Mozart or a Rossini should delight the ear. — Alexis Soyer, The Modern Housewife 1851

Marinara Sauce
makes 1 quart

1/4 c.	olive oil
1/2 c.	yellow onion, finely chopped
4	cloves garlic, peeled and crushed
1	bay leaf
1/4 tsp.	cinnamon
1/2 tsp.	salt
1/4 tsp.	white pepper
4 c.	ripe tomatoes, deseeded and chopped
1 c.	tomato paste
1/2 c.	white wine
1/4 c.	fresh basil, chopped
1/4 c.	fresh oregano, chopped

Saute the onion and garlic in the olive oil. Add all of the other ingredients and simmer over a medium heat until thickened, approximately 45 minutes. Remove the bay leaf. Puree and strain the sauce.

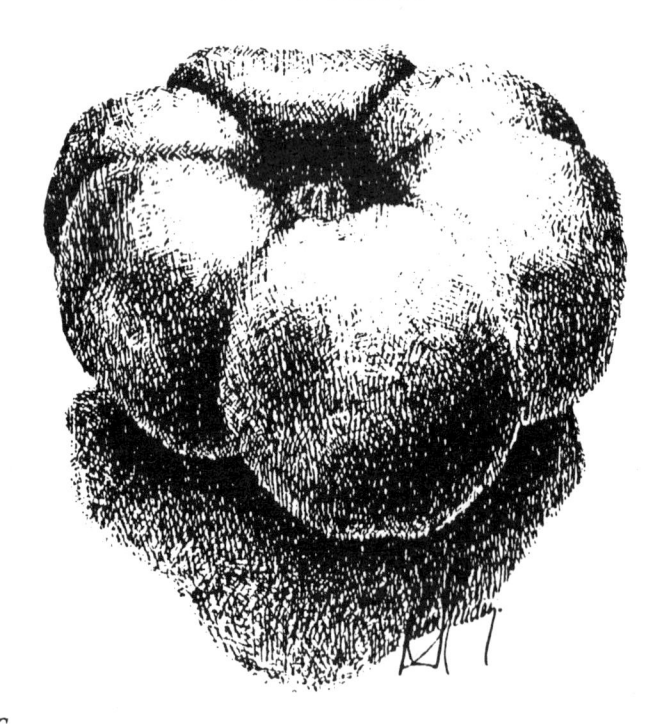

This barbecue sauce is excellent for traditional barbecue uses and also as a marinade for tofu, tempeh and vegetables. Try using leftover barbecue sauce in our famous bean soup (see recipe page 69).

Barbecue Sauce
makes 1 1/2 quarts

1/4 c.	unsalted butter, melted
2 c.	yellow onions, chopped
4	cloves garlic, peeled and minced
1 c.	orange juice
2 Tbsp.	raisins
1/4 c.	cider vinegar
2 Tbsp.	peanut oil
2 Tbsp.	orange zest, chopped
2 c.	molasses
2 c.	tomato puree
4 tsp.	paprika
1/4 tsp.	allspice
2 tsp.	dijon mustard
2 tsp.	worcestershire sauce
2 tsp.	crushed red chilies
2 tsp.	salt

Saute the onions, and garlic in the butter. Puree the raisins with the orange juice, vinegar, oil, and zest. Blend all the remaining ingredients together. Heat gently for 45 minutes over a medium heat to blend the flavors.

I consider this Indonesian recipe to be the ultimate dipping sauce. We generally serve it with our grilled chicken or tempeh satay, but stirred into other dishes, it evokes Asian flavors. Try it in our Thai chicken salad. And don't forget the value of leftovers! This sauce inspired an African peanut soup (see recipe page 56) that customers clamor for.

Spicy Peanut Sauce
makes 1 quart

1 1/2 c.	peanut butter
1/2 c.	brown sugar
2 Tbsp.	crushed red chilies
2 c.	orange-tamari sauce (see recipe page 205)

Combine all of the ingredients until smooth. Heat gently to serve as a hot dipping sauce, adding water if necessary to thin and make a smoother sauce.

Seeing is deceiving. It's eating that's believing. — James Thurber, Further Fables for Our Time 1956

Pomegranate-walnut sauce is typically used in Soviet Georgian cuisine. It is an absolutely delicious marinade and finishing sauce for grilled chicken, fish, tofu or tempeh. This sauce is a wonderful addition to cooked vegetables or dolloped on baked potatoes. Blend with sour cream or yogurt for a lighter and much richer tasting sauce.

Pomegranate-Walnut Sauce
makes a little over 1 quart

1/2 c.	yellow onions, chopped
1 tsp.	ground tumeric
1/2 c.	chicken or vegetable stock, or water
2 c.	walnuts, toasted and finely ground
2 c.	pomegranate juice
2 Tbsp.	lemon juice
1 tsp.	fructose or sugar
1	cinnamon stick
1/4 tsp.	ground cardamom
1/8 tsp.	white pepper
1/4 tsp.	salt

Combine all of the ingredients together in a saucepan and simmer over low heat for 45 minutes. Stir often to prevent sticking. Serve hot.

Mornay Sauce
makes 1 pint

1/4 c.	unsalted butter, melted
1/4 c.	all-purpose flour
1 c.	milk, heated
1 Tbsp.	dijon mustard
2 Tbsp.	Parmesan cheese
1/4 c.	grated cheese such as jack cheddar, Swiss or gruyere
1/4 tsp.	nutmeg
1/4 tsp.	pepper
1/2 tsp.	salt

Make a roux with the butter and flour and simmer for five minutes, whisking often. Stir in the hot milk and whisk quickly to create a thick white sauce. Add the remaining ingredients and heat until the cheese is completely melted. Thin with hot water or milk to the desired consistency.

Gourmets dig their graves with their teeth. — French proverb

Mushroom Sauce
makes 1 quart

2 Tbsp.	butter or canola oil
4 c.	mushrooms, sliced
1/2 c.	yellow onion, finely chopped
1/4 c.	dry sherry
2 tbsp.	tamari or soy sauce
1/4 c.	unsalted butter
1/4 c.	all-purpose flour
2 c.	milk, heated

Saute the mushrooms and onions in the 2 tbsp. of butter or oil until tender. Stir in the sherry and tamari and simmer for five minutes to evaporate the alcohol. Make a roux with the butter and flour and whisk constantly over a medium heat for three minutes. Stir in the hot milk and whisk quickly to create a smooth, thickened sauce. Stir in the sauteed mushrooms and heat gently to blend the flavors. Add salt and pepper to taste.

Cilantro Sour Cream
makes 1 pint

1 c.	sour cream
1/2 c.	plain lowfat yogurt
1/2 c.	fresh cilantro leaves, chopped
1/8 tsp.	Tabasco sauce
1/4 tsp.	salt

Blend all of the ingredients well and chill.

joe saxe

This is a classic recipe for pesto sauce, and I can't think of any way to improve upon it. If pinenuts are hard to find or prohibitively expensive, substitute walnuts. Pesto sauce keeps well in the refrigerator for up to two weeks. It may be frozen for up to one year, but I recommend blending it in a food processor or blender once it is thawed to regain its smooth texture.

Pesto Sauce
makes 1 quart

3	cloves garlic, peeled
1/2 c.	pine nuts, toasted
1/2 c.	Parmesan cheese, grated
1/2 tsp.	salt
1/8 tsp.	white pepper
2 c.	basil, washed and blotted dry
1/2 c.	olive oil
1/4 c.	water

Blend the first 5 ingredients together in a food processor. Add the basil leaves and blend until smooth with the olive oil. Add the water to thin the sauce, if necessary.

Good oil, like good wine, is a gift from the gods. The grape and the olive are among the priceless benefactions of the soil, and were destined, each in its way, to promote the welfare of man. — George Ellwanger, Pleasures of the Table 1903

Roasted Red Pepper Sauce
makes 1 quart

3	red bell peppers
2 Tbsp.	olive oil
1/2 c.	yellow onion, sliced
1 tsp.	salt
1/4 tsp.	white pepper
1 c.	water

Roast the peppers by holding over an open gas or charcoal flame with tongs, or by placing in a 400 degree oven for 30 minutes. Turn the peppers frequently to roast on all sides. The skin should be blackened all over. Peel, remove membranes and seeds, and puree the peppers in a food processor or blender. Saute the onion in the olive oil for 5 minutes, cool and puree. Add the salt, pepper, and water to the pureed peppers and onion to create a smooth sauce. Simmer over low heat, stirring often to prevent sticking.

Sauces & Condiments

Tartar Sauce
Makes over 1 pint

3 1/2 c.	mayonnaise
1/4 c.	capers
1/4 c.	yellow onion, finely chopped
1/4 c.	kosher pickle, finely chopped
2 Tbsp.	fresh dill, chopped

Blend all ingredients well. Keep refrigerated.

Cranberry Ketchup

Makes 1 quart

1 lb.	cranberries, washed well
1 c.	fructose or sugar
1 c.	cider vinegar
1 tsp.	white pepper
1 tsp.	cloves
1 tsp.	dry mustard
1 c.	onions, chopped
2 tsp.	cinnamon
1 Tbsp.	salt
1/2 c.	fresh horseradish, grated

Cook the cranberries in the vinegar with the sugar until soft. Add all of the other ingredients and heat to a boil. Reduce the heat and simmer for 30 min. Puree and strain the ketchup and simmer to reduce by almost half. Heat pack the ketchup in canning jars at this point or store in the refrigerator in glass containers. This recipe keeps for a miraculously long time in the refrigerator.

Country Fare. Much more than food!! — a customer

Sauces & Condiments

Nectarine Mustard
makes 1 quart

3	large nectarines, peeled and chopped
1 c.	yellow mustard powder
1 c.	cold water
1/2 Tbsp.	orange zest, finely chopped
1 c.	white wine or champagne vinegar
1 c.	fructose or sugar
1 Tbsp.	salt
1/4 c.	lemon juice

Simmer the nectarines for about 5 minutes, stirring often, until the fruit become soft and releases the juice. Add the remaining ingredients and simmer until thickened, about 1 1/2 hours, stirring occasionally to prevent sticking. At this point you may can the mustard in glass canning jars using a traditional hot water bath, or refrigerate it for up to 3 weeks.

This sauce is delicious served hot with potato pancakes or French toast.

Apple Sauce
makes 1 quart

4	large, tart, organic apples such as Pippin or Granny Smith
1 c.	brown sugar
1 tsp.	cinnamon
1/2 tsp.	nutmeg
1/4 tsp.	allspice
1/4 tsp.	ground cloves
1/2 tsp.	ground ginger powder

Peel, core, chop, and cook the apples in a little water over medium heat in a heavy-bottomed sauce pan for about 45 minutes. Mash well while still hot. Stir in all of the other ingredients. Store in the refrigerator for up to two weeks.

Sauces & Condiments

Honey yogurt sauce is delightful addition to a fresh fruit platter. Use it as a dessert sauce for almond bread pudding, quince dumplings or Russian honeycake.

Honey Yogurt Sauce
makes 1 pint

- 1 c.   plain lowfat yogurt
- 1/4 c   honey
- 1 tsp.   vanilla extract
- 1/2 c.   lowfat sour cream
- 1/4 c.   mayonnaise

Whisk all ingredients together and chill.

We use red onion marmalade at the restaurant almost exclusively with our sweet potato pancakes. This savory/sweet condiment is also delicious on a grilled vegetarian sandwich consisting of tart apples, walnut butter and cheddar cheese. It sounds strange, but the flavors are exceptional together. Red onion marmalade will keep for months in the refrigerator.

Red Onion Marmalade
makes a little over 1 quart

3 c.	red onions, thinly sliced
2 Tbsp.	unsalted butter
1/4 c.	red wine
1/4 c.	fructose or sugar
1/4 c.	orange juice
1 Tbsp.	orange zest

Saute the red onions in the butter until soft, about 10 minutes. Add the remaining ingredients and simmer for 45 minutes until very soft and thickened. Stir often to prevent sticking.

Onion: humble kindred of the lily clan, rooted from oblivion by Alexander the Great and bestrewn by him, along with learning, to the civilized world, thus lending a touch of wisdom and sophistication to the whole. — Della Lutes, The Country Kitchen 1938

Sauces & Condiments

Raspberry-Rhubarb Conserves
makes approximately 1 quart

2	1/2 pint baskets raspberries, washed and drained
1	12 inch stalk rhubarb, washed well and sliced into 1/2 inch lengths (about 2 c.)
1 1/2 c.	fructose or 2 c. sugar
1/2 tsp.	cinnamon

Simmer the rhubarb and fructose or sugar in a heavy-bottomed pot for thirty-five minutes or until rhubarb begins to fall apart. Stir in the raspberries and cinnamon and continue to simmer stirring well to create a thick sauce, approximately twenty-five minutes. Hot pack in glass jars or refrigerate immediately. This conserve will keep 4 weeks or so refrigerated.

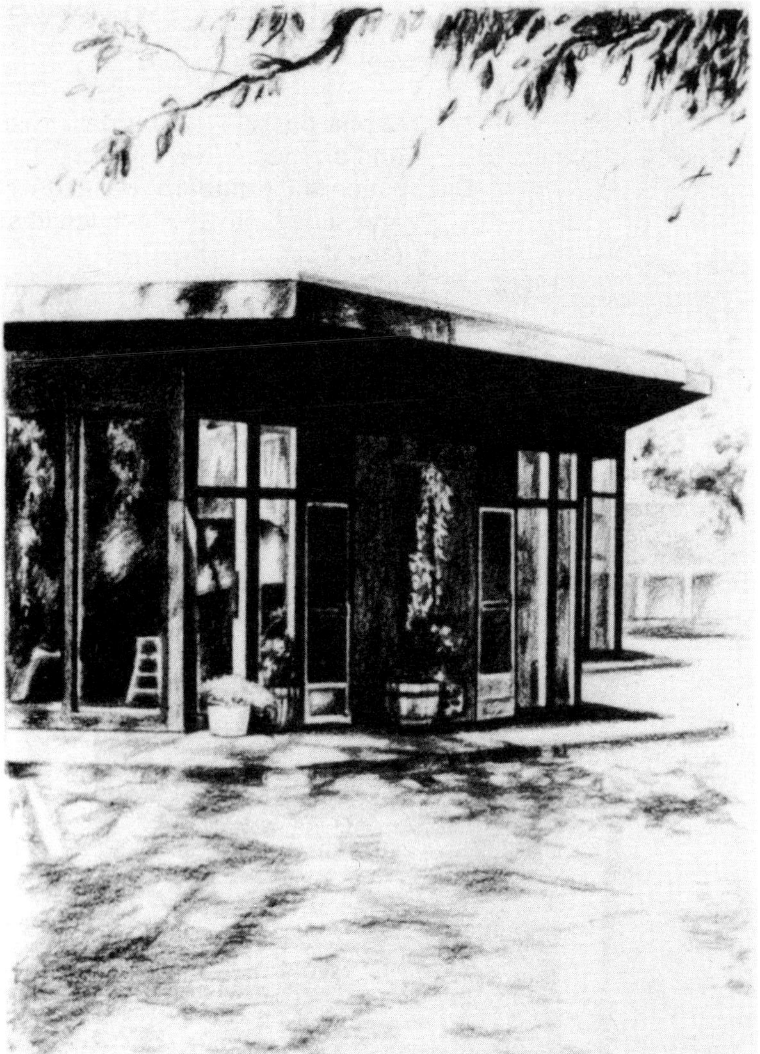

Desserts

Oatmeal Chocolate Chip Cookies	226
Vanilla Chip Cookies	227
Lemon Squares	228
Blackberry Bars	229
Oat Date Bars	230
Thumbprint Cookies	231
Ginger Snaps	232
Pecan Pie Cookies	233
Apple Butter Bars	234
Pistachio-Coconut Cookies	235
Nan's Walnut Horns	236
Russian Tea Cakes	237
Peanut Butter Middles	238
Almond Rocca Cookies	239
Holstein Brownies	240
White Chocolate Brownies	241
Creme de Menthe Brownies	242
Perfect Pie Pastry	243
French Apple Pie	244
Blueberry Pie	245
Carob-Walnut Pie	246
Mango-Raspberry Crisp	247
Carrot Cake	248
Russian Honey Cake	250
Almond Bread Pudding	251
Organic Fruitcake	252
Quince Dumplings	254
Baked Apple with Dried Fruit	256

Desserts

Most of our customers are so satiated after eating lunch or dinner that just a little bite of something sweet is sufficient for dessert. That is not to contradict that many are able to demolish a piece of carrot cake or pie after consuming an entire entree, soup, a salad and several beverages (these, quite naturally, are our favorite customers)! Nevertheless, you will notice that the majority of the recipes in the dessert chapter fall under the realm of "cookie."

Our best seller!

Oatmeal Chocolate Chip Cookies
Makes 2 dozen cookies

1/2 c.	butter, softened
3/4 c.	brown sugar
1	eggs
1/2 tsp.	vanilla
3/4 c.	unbleached flour
1 1/4 c.	rolled oats
3/4 tsp.	baking soda
1/4 tsp.	salt
1 1/2 c.	chocolate chips

Cream the butter and sugar together. Beat in the eggs and vanilla. Add the flour, oats, baking soda, and salt. Stir in the chocolate chips. Chill for one hour before baking. Scoop dough in 2 Tbsp. portions and flatten slightly on an ungreased cookie sheet. Bake at 350 degrees for 12 minutes.

Desserts

Vanilla Chip Cookies
Makes 24 cookies

1/2 c.	unsalted butter, softened
2/3 c.	fructose or sugar
1	egg
1 tsp.	vanilla
1 1/2 c.	unbleached flour
6 Tbsp.	cocoa
1/2 tsp.	baking soda
1/4 tsp.	salt
1/2 c.	pecans, toasted and chopped
1/2 c.	vanilla chips

Cream the butter and sugar together. Add the egg and vanilla and beat until fluffy. Stir together the dry ingredients. Blend with the creamed mixture until smooth. Stir in the pecans and vanilla chips. Shape into rolls and chill until firm. Slice the rolls into 1/2 inch pieces and place on a parchment paper-lined cookie sheet. Bake at 350 degrees for 8 to 10 minutes.

Lemon Squares
Makes 12 cookies

3/4 c.	unsalted butter, softened
6 Tbsp.	confectioner's sugar
1 1/2 c.	unbleached flour
3	eggs
1 c.	fructose or sugar
3 Tbsp.	unbleached flour
1/8 tsp.	salt
1 tsp.	baking powder
1/3 c.	lemon juice

Blend the confectioner's sugar, flour, and butter in a food processor. Press into a baking pan. Bake at 350 degrees for 10 minutes. Beat the eggs and remaining ingredients in a food processor. Pour over the cookie crust. Bake at 350 degrees for an additional 25 minutes.

...the lemon squares I would beg, borrow and steal for! — Lamont

Blackberry Bars
Serves 12

1 1/4 c.	almonds
1 1/2 c.	unbleached flour
3/4 c.	brown sugar
3/4 c.	unsalted butter
1/2 tsp.	vanilla extract
3/4 c.	blackberry preserves

Chop the almonds with the steel blade of a food processor until coarsely chopped. Process these almonds with the flour, sugar, butter, and vanilla until the mixture resembles coarse crumbs. Save 1 c. of the crumb mixture and press the remaining crumbs into an ungreased pan. Spread the preserves over the crust and sprinkle with the reserved crumbs pressing lightly to set. Bake in preheated 350 degree oven until brown, about thirty minutes.

Oat Date Bars
makes 1 dozen

3 c.	dates, pitted
1 c.	apple juice
1/2 c.	water
3/4 c.	soy margarine
1/2 c.	brown sugar
1 1/2 c.	whole wheat flour
1 1/2 c.	rolled oats
1 1/2 tsp.	baking powder

Simmer the dates, juice and water together over medium heat until soft, about 15 minutes. Mash or puree the mixture and set aside to cool. Combine the margarine, brown sugar, oats, flour and baking powder. Press half of the oat mixture evenly in a baking pan. Spread the date puree evenly over the crust. Sprinkle the remaining crust mixture over the dates and press lightly. Bake at 350 degrees for 40 minutes or until lightly browned. Allow to cool and firm up before cutting into squares.

Thumbprint Cookies
Makes 2 dozen cookies

3 c.	walnuts, finely chopped
1 c.	unsalted butter, softened
2/3 c.	fructose
2 c.	unbleached flour
1 tsp.	baking powder
1 tsp.	cinnamon
1/4 tsp.	salt
2	eggs, separated with the whites lightly beaten and set aside
1 tsp.	vanilla
1 Tbsp.	lemon zest, finely chopped
1/2 c.	raspberry or apricot jam

Stir together the flour, 1 c. of the chopped walnuts, baking powder, cinnamon, salt and lemon zest. Cream the butter and sugar together. Beat in the egg yolks, then the vanilla. Stir in the flour mixture. Measure the dough in 2 tsp. portions and roll into balls. Roll each ball in the egg white and then in the 1 c. of chopped walnuts. Place on a parchment paper-lined baking sheet and make a "thumbprint" in each cookie. Fill the depression with 1/4 tsp. of jam. Bake cookies at 350 degrees for 20 minutes.

Ginger Snaps
makes 2 dozen cookies

2 c.	unsalted butter, melted
3 c.	molasses
1 c.	fructose or sugar
9 c.	all purpose flour
4 tsp.	salt
4 tsp.	baking soda
4 tsp.	ground ginger powder
1/2 c.	powdered sugar

Cream the butter, molasses, and sugar in a kitchen mixer. Stir in the remaining ingredients. Chill the dough overnight. Roll the dough into 1 ounce balls and flatten slightly on a parchment papered cookie sheet. Bake at 350 degrees for 8 minutes. When cool, sprinkle with powdered sugar.

I love your ginger snaps! They're delicious! — Sincerely, Ruth Selby

Pecan Pie Cookies

Makes 12 cookies

Crust

1 1/3 c.	unbleached flour
2 Tbsp.	brown sugar
1/2 c.	unsalted butter, softened

Blend all of the ingredients together and press into a baking pan. Bake at 350 degrees for 12 minutes.

Topping

2	eggs
1/2 c.	corn syrup
2 Tbsp.	melted butter
1 tsp.	vanilla
1/8 tsp.	salt

Blend all of the ingredients together in a food processor. Stir in:

3 c. chopped pecans

Pour the topping over the baked crust and bake for 20 minutes more at 350 degrees.

Apple Butter Bars
makes 1 dozen bars

1 1/2 c.	apple butter
1 Tbsp.	lemon juice
2	eggs
1 1/2 c.	fructose or sugar
2 c.	dates, pitted and chopped
3/4 c.	safflower or canola oil
2 1/2 c.	all-purpose flour
2 tsp.	baking soda
1 tsp.	cinnamon
1 tsp.	nutmeg
1/4 tsp.	ground cloves

Blend the apple butter with the eggs, lemon juice, sugar, dates and oil. Stir together the dry ingredients. Stir the dry ingredients into the wet ingredients just until blended. Spread the batter in a greased and floured baking pan. Bake at 350 degrees for 25 minutes. Sprinkle with powdered sugar. Cut into bars 2 inches by 3 inches.

Pistachio-Coconut Cookies
makes 2 dozen delectable confections

3 1/3 c.	shelled, raw pistachios
2 c.	powdered sugar
2 c.	shredded coconut
1 c.	unsalted butter, softened
2	eggs
1 tsp.	vanilla extract
1 1/3 c.	all-purpose flour
1 tsp.	baking soda
1/2 tsp.	salt

Process the pistachios in a food processor until finely chopped. Add the coconut and process for 1 minute more. Set aside. Blend the sugar, butter, egg, and vanilla in a kitchen mixer. Add the flour, baking soda and salt, and blend well. Stir in the powdered pistachios and coconut. Drop by tablespoonfuls on a parchment paper-lined baking sheet. Bake at 350 degrees for 12 minutes or until delightfully green-golden.

Nan's Walnut Horns
Makes 40 cookies

Dough

2 1/4	unbleached flour
1 c.	unsalted butter, softened
1/2 c.	sour cream or plain lowfat yogurt
1 c.	lowfat cottage cheese

Filling

1 c.	fructose or sugar
1 tsp.	cinnamon
1 Tbsp.	unsalted butter, melted
1/2 c.	raisins
1/2 c.	walnuts, toasted and chopped

Mix the butter and flour in a food processor. Add the sour cream and cottage cheese and process just until blended. Divide the dough into 4 balls and wrap in plastic wrap. Refrigerate overnight. Mix the filling ingredients together. Roll one ball of dough into a thin 6" diameter circle and sprinkle evenly with 3 Tbsp. of filling. Keep the remaining dough refrigerated until ready to roll out. Cut into 10 pie-shaped wedges. Roll each wedge from the wide edge to the point. Place on an ungreased cookie sheet and bake the crescents at 375 degrees for 15-20 minutes or until brown.

It is extremely easy to eat too many of these melt-in-your-mouth delights. Don't say I didn't warn you!

Russian Tea Cakes

makes 2 dozen cookies

2 c.	unsalted butter, softened
1 c.	powdered sugar
4 1/2 c.	cake flour (or 4 c. unbleached flour, sifted 3 twice)
1/2 tsp.	salt
1 1/2 c.	walnuts, toasted and finely ground (powdered, actually)
2 tsp.	vanilla extract
1/2 tsp.	almond extract

Cream the softened butter and sugar in a kitchen mixer. Slowly add the flour and salt. Blend in the nuts and almond extract. Roll into 1 inch balls. Place the balls 1/2 inch apart on a parchment paper lined cookie sheet. Bake at 400 degrees for 15 minutes or until brown. Dust with powdered sugar while still warm.

We tried out these cookies with my brother, Dick, to get an unbiased opinion and a new, nifty idea for a better name. Unfortunately, no magical nomenclature emerged even after consuming countless cookies. We did gain an enthusiastic, although addicted, convert for our efforts.

Peanut Butter Middles

makes 1 dozen cookies

1 c.	all-purpose flour
1/3 c.	cocoa powder
1/3 tsp.	baking soda
1/3 c.	fructose or sugar
1/3 c.	brown sugar
1/3 c.	unsalted butter, softened
1/4 c.	peanut butter
1 tsp.	vanilla extract
1	egg

Filling:

1/2 c.	peanut butter
1/2 c.	powdered sugar

Blend the dry ingredients (except the sugars) together. Beat the butter, peanut butter, and sugars together until fluffy. Add the vanilla and egg. Stir in the flour mixture. In a separate bowl, combine the peanut butter and powdered sugar well. Roll the filling into 1 inch balls. Shape 2 tablespoons of the chocolate cookie dough around the filling balls with floured hands. Place the cookies 2 inches apart on a parchment-papered baking sheet. Flatten with the bottom of a glass dipped in sugar or fructose. Bake at 350 degrees for 12 minutes.

These were my favorite cookies as a child. My mom made big batches of them for special occasions and froze the extras for upcoming family get-togethers. (They taste great frozen!)

Almond Rocca Cookies
makes 2 dozen scrumptious bites

1 c.	unsalted butter, softened
1 c.	brown sugar
2 c.	unbleached flour
1/2 tsp.	baking soda
1 tsp.	baking powder
1 tsp.	vanilla extract
1 1/2 c.	chocolate chips
1 c.	almonds, toasted and finely chopped

Blend the butter and sugar together well. Stir together the flour, baking soda and powder. Add to the creamed butter and sugar with the vanilla. Press the dough into a shallow baking pan and bake at 275 degrees for 40 minutes. Sprinkle the chocolate over the hot baked cookie bar and spread evenly over the surface like frosting. Sprinkle with the chopped almonds. Cut into 24 squares while still warm.

Holstein Brownies
serves 12

1 c.	semisweet chocolate, chopped
1/2 c.	unsalted butter
1 1/2 c.	fructose or sugar
4	eggs, beaten
2 tsp.	vanilla extract
1 c.	unbleached flour
1 c.	walnuts, toasted and chopped
1 c.	cream cheese, softened
1/2 c.	fructose or sugar
2	eggs
2 Tbsp.	unbleached flour

Melt the chocolate and butter in a double boiler. Stir well and cool. Stir in the fructose, eggs, and vanilla. Beat in the flour and nuts. Spread in a buttered baking pan. Blend the cream cheese, fructose, eggs and flour until smooth. Spoon the cream cheese mixture over the brownie dough in the pan and stir in gently to marbleize. Bake at 350 degrees for 35 minutes. Do not overbake!! Cool in the pan before cutting into bars.

White Chocolate Brownies
Makes 12 large brownies

1/4 c.	unsalted butter
1/2 c.	Amaretto
1 c.	white chocolate, grated
5	eggs
1 tsp.	vanilla
1/2 tsp.	almond extract
1/4 tsp.	salt
1 c.	fructose or sugar
1 c.	unbleached flour
1 c.	almonds, blanched, toasted and chopped

Line a 9x13x2 inch pan with parchment and butter well. Melt butter and stir in Amaretto. Add white chocolate and whisk until smooth. Beat eggs until fluffy, add vanilla and almond extracts, salt and then sugar, a little at a time. Beat at high speed until thick. Fold in the chocolate mixture, then the flour and finally the almonds. Pour batter into the prepared pan and bake for 25 minutes at 375 degrees. Cool in pan for 15 minutes before cutting.

Note: Frost white chocolate brownies with cream cheese frosting (see recipe page 249) or melted white chocolate for an even richer treat.

Creme de Menthe Brownies
serves 12

2 c.	fructose or sugar
1 c.	pecans, toasted and chopped
1/2 c.	unbleached flour
1/2 c.	cocoa powder
3	eggs
3 Tbsp.	creme de menthe
1 tsp.	vanilla extract
1 c.	unsalted butter, melted

Icing:

2 Tbsp.	semi-sweet chocolate, chopped
1 Tbsp.	unsalted butter, softened
1 Tbsp.	creme de menthe
1 Tbsp.	milk
1 tsp.	vanilla extract
1 c.	powdered sugar

Blend the fructose, pecans, flour, and cocoa powder together. Blend the eggs, creme de menthe, vanilla. and melted butter together. Combine the dry ingredients with the wet ingredients. Pour into a buttered pan and bake at 350 degrees for 45 minutes.

For the icing:

Melt the chocolate in a double boiler. Cool. Combine in a mixer the chocolate, butter, creme de menthe, milk, vanilla and sugar. Spread the icing on the cooled brownies.

Perfect Pie Pastry

yields 2 pie shells or 1 double crust pie

1 c.	unsalted butter
2 1/4 c.	unbleached all-purpose flour or whole wheat pastry flour
6 Tbsp.	cold water

Grate the butter into the flour by hand. Gently blend the water in with a pastry blender or fork until the dough forms a ball. Do not overwork! The crust becomes more flaky the colder the ingredients are kept, so use your hands as little as possible to avoid warming up the butter.

Refrigerate the dough for ten minutes before rolling out to line a pie plate. Always roll the dough out to hang 1 1/2 inches over the rim. Measure the rolled out dough with an overturned pie plate. Cut the jagged edges off to form a perfect circle and gently fold twice to create a quarter wedge. Place the wedge in one quadrant of the pie plate and unfold the dough. Roll the overhanging dough under twice and press vertically to form a thick upright rim. Crimp the edges by pushing the two knuckles of your "helping hand" (the left hand if you're right-handed) into the outer edge and the knuckle of your "shaping hand" from the inside edge into the space between the two knuckles. Continue around the rim of the pie until the entire edge is crimped. Shape gently with your hands to create an even, upright, fluted crust.

For a double crust pie, do not form an upright rim on the lower crust, but let the dough hang over. Fill the pie and place the second dough circle over the filling. Pinch both layers of pastry at the edges and roll both layers of dough into the upright rim and crimp as above.

French Apple Pie
serves 6

6	tart apples, peeled and sliced
1/2 c.	unbleached flour
1/2 tsp.	cinnamon
1/2 c.	fructose or sugar
1/2 c.	brown sugar
1/2 c.	unsalted butter, cut into small pieces
1 1/2 c.	crumb topping (see recipe page 19)

Blend the flour, cinnamon, sugars, and butter pieces. Toss the apples in this mixture. Place the filling in a prepared pie shell. Sprinkle 1 cup of crumb topping over the pie. Bake at 400 degrees for 10 minutes, then lower the heat to 350 degrees and bake for 40 minutes more or until the pie pastry and crumb topping are browned.

Good apple pies are a considerable part of our domestic happiness. — Jane Austen

Blueberry Pie
serves 6

4 c.	fresh blueberries
1 1/3 c.	fructose or sugar
1/2 c.	tapioca flour or cornstarch
1/2 tsp.	cinnamon
1/3 c.	cold unsalted butter, grated
1	prepared pie crust plus extra dough for the lattice top

Mash 2 cups of the blueberries. Blend with the sugar, tapioca flour, cinnamon and butter. Simmer gently for 10 minutes to thicken. Stir in the remaining whole blueberries. Fill a prepared pie crust. Roll the remaining dough into a rectangle and cut into 10 1/2 inch strips. Weave the strips of dough on top of the pie and brush lightly with an egg wash (see recipe page 129). Bake at 425 degrees for 10 minutes then lower the heat to 375 degrees and bake for 40 minutes more.

Pie, often foolishly abused, is a good creature at the right time and in the angles of thirty and forty degrees, although in semicircles and quadrants it may sometimes prove too much for delicate stomachs. — Artemus Ward

Carob-Walnut Pie
serves 6

2 1/2 c.	carob chips, melted
1 lb.	soft tofu
1/4 c.	honey
1 c.	walnuts, toasted and chopped

Blind bake a pie shell with pie weights or dried beans on top of parchment paper at 425 degrees for 15 minutes. Remove the weights and bake at 350 degrees for 15 minutes. Blend the tofu, melted carob, and honey in a food processor. Stir in the walnuts. Pour the filling into the cooled pie shell and chill for 2 hours before slicing.

Mango-Raspberry Crisp
Makes 8 delectable servings

4	large fresh mangoes, sliced
4 c.	fresh raspberries
3/4 c.	all purpose flour
1 c.	brown sugar
1/2 tsp.	cinnamon

Topping:

2 c.	old-fashioned rolled oats
3/4 c.	all purpose flour
1/2 c.	walnuts, toasted and chopped
1/4 c.	sunflower seeds
1/2 tsp.	salt
1 tsp.	cinnamon
1/2 tsp.	allspice
1/3 c.	honey
1/3 c.	unsalted butter, melted

Butter a rectangular glass baking dish. Mix the sliced mangoes with the flour, brown sugar, and cinnamon. Sprinkle the raspberries on top. Combine all of the topping ingredients together and sprinkle evenly on top of the fruit. Bake at 375 degrees for 40 minutes. Serve with vanilla ice cream or honey yogurt sauce (see recipe page 219).

There should be a restaurant like this in every community in the whole world!

Carrot Cake
serves 12

1/2 c.	whole wheat flour
2 c.	unbleached flour
1 tsp.	cinnamon
1/4 tsp.	allspice
1/2 tsp.	nutmeg
1 c.	brown sugar
2 tsp.	baking soda
1/4 tsp.	salt
3	eggs, beaten
1/4 c.	safflower or canola oil
1/3 c.	buttermilk
1 tsp.	vanilla extract
1 c.	coconut, shredded
3 c.	carrots, shredded
1 c.	pineapple, chopped and drained well
1 c.	walnuts, toasted and chopped

Blend the dry ingredients together well. Blend the wet ingredients together separately. Add the dry ingredients to the wet ingredients and mix thoroughly. Stir in the coconut, carrots, pineapple, and walnuts. Place batter in a well buttered cake pan and bake at 350 degrees for 40 minutes. When cool, frost lavishly with cream cheese frosting.

Cream Cheese Frosting

   1/2 c.   cream cheese
   1/2 c.   unsalted butter, softened
  1/2 tsp.   vanilla extract
     5 c.   powdered sugar

Blend the cream cheese, butter and vanilla together with a kitchen mixer. Gradually add the powdered sugar until a soft frosting forms. Use more sugar for a firmer frosting or add milk by the teaspoon to create a glaze.

Russian Honey Cake
serves 8

1/4 c.	unsalted butter, softened
1/2 c.	brown sugar
2 eggs,	separated
1 1/4 c.	cake flour
1 tsp.	baking soda
1/2 tsp.	baking powder
	pinch salt
1 Tbsp.	orange zest, finely chopped
1/2 c.	sour cream
1/2 tsp.	cinnamon
1/4 tsp.	nutmeg
1/4 c.	dried currants or raisins
1/2 c.	walnuts, toasted and chopped
1/2 c.	dates, pitted and chopped

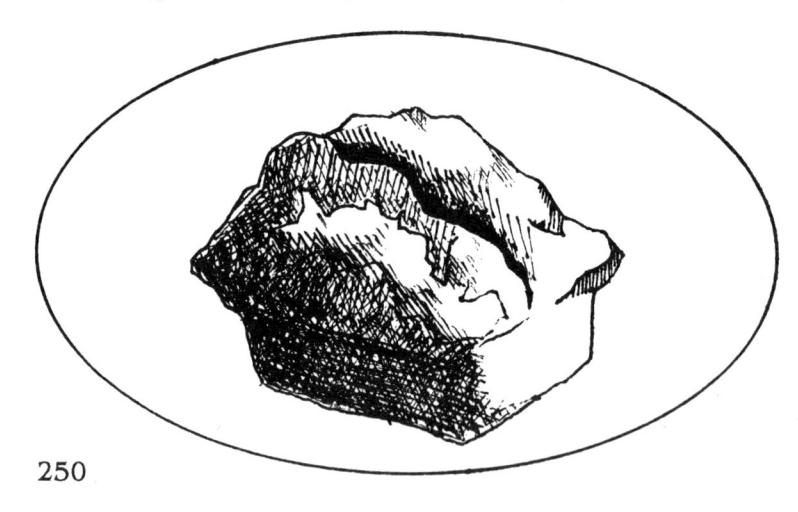

Cream the softened butter and sugar until light and fluffy, then beat in the honey. Beat in the egg yolks one at a time. Stir in the flour, baking soda, baking powder, and salt. Add the zest and sour cream, beating the batter until smooth. Stir in the cinnamon, nutmeg, currants, walnuts, and dates. Whip the egg whites until stiff and fold into the batter. Place the batter in a greased loaf pan lined with parchment paper. Bake 1 1/4 hours at 300 degrees until a toothpick inserted in the center comes out clean. Wrap in foil and age at room temperature for 2 days.

Desserts

This recipe for our frequently requested Almond Bread Pudding was printed in Gourmet Magazine's "You Asked For It" column in January of 1989. We still make gigantic pans of it at the restaurant several times a week.

Almond Bread Pudding
6 generous servings

1/2 c.	chopped almonds
10	almond-filled or plain croissants
4	eggs, beaten
1 c.	fructose or sugar
2 c.	milk
1/2 tsp.	almond extract
1/2 tsp.	vanilla extract
	pinch salt

Slice the croissants crosswise and place carefully in a buttered baking pan, cut-side up. Blend all of the remaining ingredients together well and pour evenly over the croissant slices. Press down all over the surface of the pudding and let stand for 10 minutes. Press the surface again to allow the croissants to soak up the batter evenly. Sprinkle with 1/2 c. of chopped almonds and bake at 350 degrees for 30 minutes.

Oh, that bread pudding! Be still, oh my heart! — Dana

The proof of the pudding is in the eating. — Henry Glapthorne, The Hollander 1635

Organic Fruitcake
makes 2 heavenly fruitcakes

3/4 c.	dried organic apricots
1 c.	dried cranberries
1 c.	dried cherries
1 c.	organic applesauce (see recipe page 218)
1 c.	organic dates, chopped
3/4 c.	orange juice
1 c.	organic apple juice
2 c.	organic whole wheat flour
1 tsp.	nutmeg
1 tsp.	cinnamon
1 tsp.	allspice
1/2 tsp.	cloves
1 tsp.	baking powder
1/2 tsp.	baking soda
1 tsp.	salt
3	eggs
1/3 c.	canola oil
1 1/2 Tbsp.	lemon zest
1 1/2 Tbsp.	orange zest
1 tsp.	vanilla
1 c.	pecans, toasted and coarsely chopped
1 c.	walnuts, toasted and coarsely chopped

Butter parchment paper and line two 8"x 4" bread pans thoroughly with the parchment paper, buttered side up. Cook the dried fruits in the orange and apple juices for 10 minutes. Cover the pan to rehydrate the fruit for an additional 10 minutes. Drain and reserve the juice in a 1 cup measure.

Combine the dry ingredients. Beat the wet ingredients together along with the juice. Stir the dry mixture into the wet mixture. Blend in the zests, cooked fruit, applesauce and nuts. Spread this thick batter in the lined pans.

Place the filled pans on the bottom rack of a 300 degree oven and bake for 1 3/4 hours or until an inserted knife comes out clean. Let the cakes cool to room temperature before removing them from the pans.

Wrap the fruitcakes in cheesecloth and drizzle liberally with brandy, amaretto or kirsch. Wrap the soaked cakes in foil and set aside in a cool place. Moisten the cakes once a week with approximately 1/2 c. liquor each for 3 weeks. Allow the cakes to age without additional liquor for 2 weeks before serving.

Quince are not an oft used fruit and rather difficult to find in ordinary markets. If you do chance upon this extraordinary fruit, try baking it in these simple but luscious dumplings. Any firm fruit such as apples, pears or even peaches may be substituted.

Quince Dumplings
makes 6 dumplings

3	quince, peeled and cored
3/4 c.	crumb topping (see recipe page 19)

Dough:

2 c.	all purpose flour
2 1/2 tsp.	baking powder
1/2 tsp.	salt
3/4 c.	cold unsalted butter
3/4 c.	milk

Syrup:

2 c.	brown sugar
2 c.	water
1/4 tsp.	cinnamon
1/4 tsp.	nutmeg
2 Tbsp.	cold butter

For the dough:

Blend the dry ingredients together. Grate the butter into the dry ingredients and mix well. Stir in the milk to form a soft dough.

(continued)

For the syrup:

Simmer the sugar, water and spices together for 20 minutes or until thickened. Stir in the cold butter. Strain the syrup before pouring over the dumplings.

To assemble:

Stuff the middle of each quince with 2 Tbsp. of the crumb topping. Roll the dough out into 6 5" rounds leaving a thick bump in the center of each. Place the fruit round side down firmly in the thick center and fold the flaps in to create a square package. Place the dumplings round side up in a shallow baking pan and pour the strained syrup over each. Bake at 375 degrees for 15 minutes. Baste with the syrup from the pan and bake an additional 20 minutes or until browned. Serve warm with ice cream.

The following dessert is foolproof and delicious. Try it with Bartlett pears or quince in place of the apples. Use kirschwasser with dried cherries, creme de cassis with dried blueberries and amaretto with the dates.

Baked Apple with Dried Fruit
serves 2

2	large, tart cooking apples
1/4 c.	dried cherries, blueberries or dates
1/4 c.	crumb topping (see recipe page 19)
1/4 c.	kirsch, creme de cassis or amaretto

Core the apples and fill with the dried fruit. Sprinkle the crumb topping on top and carefully pour the liqueur over the topping. Place in an oven-proof dish and cover well. Bake the apples at 350 degrees for 45 minutes. Serve hot with ice cream or lowfat frozen yogurt.

All millionaires love a baked apple. — Ronald Firbank

Index

Acorn Squash with Walnuts Soup, 67
African Peanut Soup, 56
Almond Bread Pudding, 251
Apple Sauce, 218
Apple, Baked with Dried Fruit, 256
Asian Rice Salad, 108
Aztec Black Bean Salad, 92

Barbecue Sauce, 207
Barbecued Bean Soup, 69
Barley Mushroom Soup, 59
Barley Pilaf, 194
Bars
　Apple Butter, 234
　Blackberry, 229
　Lemon Squares, 228
　Oat-date, 230
　Pecan Pie Cookies, 233
Beer and Cheese Soup with Pecans, 79
Beet Borscht, 58
Black-eyed Pea with Greens Soup, 75
Blintzes, 51
Blueberry Turnovers, 30
Boursin, 155
Boursin Dip, 156
Brownies
　Creme de Menthe, 242
　Holstein, 240
　White Chocolate, 241
Bstilla, 170
Burger
　Falafel, 136
　Turkey, 134
　Veggie, 135

Cabbage, Stuffed, 172
Cake
　Carrot, 248
　Fruit, Organic, 252
　Russian Honey, 250
　Russian Tea, 237
Carrot Salad with Honey Yogurt Dressing, 95
Cashew Fried Rice, 49
Cheesecake, Breakfast Savory, 46
Chicken
　Adobo, 178
　Grilled Breast of, 132
　Mexican Chicken Pie, 192
　Oven-Fried, 166
　Pecan Baked, 151
　Pecan Crisp, 181
　Salad with Toasted Almonds, 122
Chili, White Bean, 179
Chutney
　Cranberry, 202
　Mango, 201
Cilantro Sour Cream, 212
Cinnamon-Brandied Apples, 125
Coffeecake, Blackberry Sour Cream, 35
Coleslaw
　Buttermilk, 93
　Spicy Red, 94
Cookies
　Almond Rocca, 239
　Ginger Snaps, 232
　Nan's Walnut Horns, 236
　Oatmeal Chocolate Chip, 226
　Peanut Butter Middles, 238
　Pistachio-Coconut, 235
　Thumbprint, 231
　Vanilla Chip, 227
Couscous Salad, 98
Cranberry Ketchup, 216
Cream of Carrot with Amaretto Soup, 77
Cream of Green Apple Soup, 82
Cream of Pumpkin Soup, 78
Cream of Spinach with Feta Cheese Soup, 80
Creamy Turkey Garbonzo Soup, 84
Crepes, 50
Crumb Topping, 19
Curried Rice Salad, 106

Curried Tomato Vegetable Soup, 68

Dahl, 70
Dijon Dip, 157
Dip
    Boursin, 156
    Dijon, 157
Dolmas, 150
Dressing
    Garlic Herb, 112
    Rasberry Vinaigrette, 113

Egg
    Hard Boiled, 121
    Salad, 120
Eggplant
    Baked Stuffed, 189
    Caviar, 149
    Melitzanopita, 188
    Salad, Savory, 101
Eggs
    Baked in a Tomato Nest, 52
Empanadas, 126

Fajitas, Vegetarian, 131
Falafel Patties, 136
French Toast
    Batter, 36
    Hawaiian, 37
    Pistachio, 38

Garlic Spread, Roasted, 160
Gingered Rice Soup, 66
Grandma C's Potato Salad, 97
Greek Feta Salad, 99
Guacamole, 162

Hummus, 118

Lasagne Verde, 168
Lemon Curd, 33
Lentil and Lovage Soup, 71

Macho Gazpacho, 57
Mango Raspberry Crisp, 247
Maple Pecan Rolls, 28
Marinara Sauce, 206

Mediterranean Vegetable Soup, 63
Melitzanopita, 188
Mexican Double Bean Soup, 73
Miso Vegetable Soup, 60
Mornay Sauce, 210
Muffins
    Apple Crumb, 18
    Banana Walnut, 24
    Bran Raisin, 27
    Oatmeal with Fruit, 26
    Orange Poppyseed, 20
    Persimmon-Ginger, 23
    Pumpkin, 22
    Zucchini, 25
Mushroom Noodle Soup, 65
Mushroom Sauce, 211

Nan's Lukshen Kugel, 185
Navy Bean with Smoked Chicken Soup, 88
Nectarine Mustard, 217

Omelette
    White Bean, 43
Orange Bean Salad, 105
Orange-Tamari Sauce, 205

Pancakes
    Blue Cornmeal, 42
    Buckwheat, 41
    Oatmeal, 40
    Potato, 47
    Pumpkin, 39
Peanut Sauce, Spicy, 208
Pear, Cashew and Blue Cheese Salad, 103
Pesto Pasta Salad, 102
Pesto Sauce, 213
Pie
    Blueberry, 245
    Carob-Walnut, 246
    French Apple, 244
    Pastry, Perfect, 243
Piroshki
    Short Dough, 128
    Yeased Dough, 130
Pomegranate-Walnut Sauce, 209

Quince Dumplings, 254

Raita
    Cucumber, 199
    Sweet Potato, 200
Raspberry-Rhubarb Conserves, 221
Ratatouille, 167
Red Onion Marmalade, 220
Red Pepper Sauce, Roasted, 214
Red Pepper Spread, Roasted, 161
Refried Beans and Cheese Soup, 64
Risotto, Vegetarian, 180
Russian Beet Salad, 100
Russian Root Vegetable Salad, 104
Russian Vegetable Pie, 183

Salad Olivier, 110
Salmon Croquettes, 190
Salmon Salad with Capers and Dill, 124
Salsa
    Corn, 204
    Fresca, 203
Sausage and Spinach Stuffed Brioche, 140
Scalloped Potatoes, 48
Seafood Salad, 123
Sherried Cream of Mushroom Soup, 76
Shrimp Bisque, 81
Smoked Chicken Waldorf, 109
Smoked Tuna Mousse, 153
Smoked Turkey and Sweet Potato Hash, 44
Spanakopita, 139
Spicy White Bean Soup, 72
Split Pea with Mint Soup, 61
Spring Rolls, Vegetarian, 148
Stuffed Eggs, Russian Style, 147
Stuffed Mushrooms with Fresh Herbs, 146
Succotash Soup, 83
Sweet Potato Salad, 107
Sweet Potatoes, Twice-Baked, 182
Szechuan Noodles, 193

Tabbouli, 96
Tachin, 186
Tahini Sauce, 159
Tamales
    Chicken, Chilies, and Roasted Muenster Cheese, 174
    Vegetarian, 176
Tapenade, 158
Tartar Sauce, 215
Teriyaki Tofu, 152
Thai Chicken Salad, 111
Tofu
    Teriyaki, 152
Tomato with Wild Rice Soup, 62
Tortilla Stack, 191
Tsimmes, 184
Tuna Salad, 119
Turkey Black Bean Soup, 85
Turkey Burger, 134
Turkey Sausage, 137
Turkey Sausage Meatball Sandwich, 138
Turkey Stuffing Soup, 86

Veggie Burger, 135

Waffles
    Buttermilk, 34
    Gingerbread, 32

Yogurt Cheese, 154

Zest, Orange or Lemon, 21

About the Author

Cathy Sillman is the chef/owner of Country Fare Restaurant, located at 2680 Middlefield Road in Palo Alto, California. She is a self-taught cook and studies cooking methods from books collected in an extensive cookbook library. Her interest in Russian food began while studying for her bachelor's degree in Russian studies at the University of Connecticut. She is currently working on her master's degree in library science at San Jose State University. A second cookbook of recipes from the restaurant is in progress.